To the
Whitney's National Committee
fall trip to Germany, October 1, 2005
at Krings-Ernst Gallery
Doris Frohnapfel

Border Horizons

Doris Frohnapfel

Doris Frohnapfel

Border Horizons

Salon Verlag
Bergen National Academy of the Arts

Introduction

Page

This book, but also exhibitions of photographs, DVD slide shows, articles for publication,
lectures and more can all be created out of the material that I accumulated between 2002
and 2005. With reference to the "photographic", I inquired into the visibility and legibility of
images. I found the political, economical and territorial shifts in the process of the changing
definitions of the EU to be a parallel to this method of inquiry. With my focal point being
borders both old and new, as well as hard and soft, I visited and photographed frontiers and
frontier terrains throughout Europe. For a long time, I collected a lot of information about
political, economical, cultural and social changes – maps, graphics, statistics, arguments and
reports. I suggest that nowadays, nobody can set out to discover the unknown any more. All
places already have a corresponding representation in our memory. My investigations are
engaged with the intelligibility of this representation. The method I deployed used some of
the characteristics of a "case study". The "case" is Europe. As in case studies, I worked on the
"data-collection" and "descriptive material" that are needed to introduce the research situa-
tion. The "fact finding" is linked to texts and images. • The text **Borders of Perception** by [7]
Ulli Seegers connects my project to a theoretical investigation into the narrative and the abs-
tract moment in which to depict and document reality, to construct a picture and to tell a
story. • The 247 photographs of **Border Horizons** take you on a journey through Europe. [17]
All images are shot on a digital still camera. • My essay **Retour, reportage** describes some [185]
of my research, as well as some of the travel and border encounters I had whilst working on
"Border Horizons". • 63 **Picture postcards** from the 60s and 70s found in second-hand [206]
shops illustrate holiday destinations under Cold War circumstances. Back then, Western
Europeans went to Spain, Italy and France; Eastern Europeans to Yugoslavia, Poland, Roma-
nia and Bulgaria. This is an exemplary instance of European reality before 1989 and before
the enlargement of the EU. • Over a period of six years, I travelled back and forth between
Germany and Norway and experienced the installation of the Schengen border at Bergen
airport, even though Norway is not a member of the EU. For the majority of Europeans, the
physical Schengen border is far away. At passport controls in airports, the border is moved
inside the countries concerned, but we no longer hesitate as to whether we should go through
the control as EU or NON-EU citizens. Although nation states still dominate people's every-
day life, migration within Europe has taken on other dimensions. Following my question as
to how artists experience living and working in two (or more) European countries today, in
the summer and autumn of 2004 I carried out **email interviews** with **Thierry Geoffroy** [210]
(France-Denmark), **Ron Haselden** (England-France), **Tanya Ury** (England-Germany),
Anu Vahtra (Estonia-Norway), **Dan Mihaltianu** (Romania-Germany) and **Maja Bajevic**
(Bosnia and Herzegovina-France). • 108 **Web-cam photographs** that I down loaded of the [224]
Finnish-Russian border show the traffic at five Nordic frontier checkpoints. • Similarly, 71
footnotes entitled **Europe: Putting pieces together** assemble quotations from my collection [231]
of news items and give a cut-up insight into the debates of recent years. My sources were
mainly daily and weekly newspapers and the Internet, particularly www.eurozine.com which
brings together articles from different European magazines such as Le monde diplomatique,
Index on Censorship, Mittelweg 36, Samtiden, Ord&Bild, du and Transit.
I am grateful to all the contributing artists and authors; to Katharina Immekus, Barbara
Wille, Marek Kiszczuk, Heinrich Miess, Adnan Özerler from Leipzig, Berlin, Cologne and
Istanbul for their company on some of my trips; to Thomas Krings-Ernst and his sharp
awareness; to Sören Kjörup for his helpfulness and to Bergen National Academy of the Arts
for the financial support. Doris Frohnapfel, July 2005

Borders of Perception

In all languages, there exist turns of phrase that disallow word-for-word translation into other languages without the sense of what is meant becoming fundamentally altered. Thus, for example, when talk in English of what in German is called 'sich ein Bild von etwas machen' is respectively translated as 'to make oneself a picture of something', this could become completely unclear and most likely be misunderstood as artistic ambition rather than comprehended as an idiom for the individual assessment of a situation. 'Sich ein Bild von etwas machen' – the expression emphasises several aspects simultaneously, aspects that are central for the thoughts to follow here, the activity and processness of perception, its individuality as much as its constructedness. It is not by chance, however, that 'to make a picture' also stands for the process of photographing itself. And thus, just as every English speaker has fun with the somewhat naïve request from a German tourist if he or she 'could make a picture' (in the sense of 'to take a photograph') of the German tourist and company, so does the use of 'to-make-a-picture' as a means to describe the operation of the camera's shutter release also indicate emphatically the mechanisation and alienation of a concept of the image that had been formerly perception-specific.

When in 1826, Joseph Nicéphore Niepce shot what was probably the first photo, he walked for the first time the ridge between images of one's own imagining and documentary recording. Niepce captures the view from his window over the roofs of his house out into the neighboring landscape. It is precisely this unspectacular view somewhere in Burgundy that, as the hour of birth of a new medium, was to lastingly revolutionise the world of images. Thus the recording of either the environment or the landscape respectively did not just become the first photographic theme, but also determined the initial function of photography. The new image medium in the first place serves in the registration of that which is changing landscape-

Grenzen der Wahrnehmung

In allen Sprachen gibt es Wendungen, die sich nicht wörtlich in andere Sprachen übersetzen lassen, ohne daß sich der Sinn des Gemeinten grundlegend ändert. So ist beispielsweise im Englischen die Rede von "sich ein Bild machen" gänzlich unverständlich bzw. würde als "to make oneself a picture" am ehesten als künstlerische Ambition mißverstanden, denn als Idiom für die individuelle Einschätzung einer Situation aufgefaßt werden können. Sich ein Bild von etwas machen – die Wendung betont gleich mehrere Aspekte, die für die folgenden Gedanken zentral sind, die Aktivität und Prozeßhaftigkeit der Wahrnehmung, ihre Individualität sowie ihre Konstruiertheit. Nicht von ungefähr steht "ein Bild machen" aber auch für den Vorgang des Photographierens. Und so, wie jeder Englischsprachige sich über die etwas unbedarfte Bitte eines deutschen Touristen im Ausland amüsiert, ob jener von ihm und seiner Begleitung "could make a picture" (im Sinne von "to take a photograph"), so sehr deutet sich mit der Verwendung von Ein-Bild-machen für die Bedienung des Auslösers einer Kamera auch die Technisierung und Veräußerlichung des vormals wahrnehmungspezifischen Bildbegriffes an.

Als Joseph Nicéphore Niepce 1826 das wohl überhaupt erste Photo schoß, beschritt er erstmals den Grat zwischen den Bildern der eigenen Vorstellung und der dokumentarischen Aufzeichnung. Niepce hält den Blick aus seinem Fenster über die Dächer seines Hauses hinaus in die Nachbarschaft und Landschaft fest. Es ist genau dieser unspektakuläre Blick irgendwo in der Bourgogne, der als Geburtsstunde eines neuen Mediums die Welt der Bilder nachhaltig revolutionieren sollte. So wurde die Aufzeichnung der Umgebung resp. Landschaft nicht nur zum ersten photographischen Motiv, sondern bestimmte auch die anfängliche Funktion der Photographie. Das neue Bildmedium dient zunächst der Registrierung dessen, was sich landschaftlich verändert. Paul Virilio spricht über das Frühstadium der Photographie daher auch von einer "Landschaftskunst", die einen

wise. Hence, in connection to the early stage of photography, Paul Virilio also talks about a 'landscape art' that possesses a purely documentary character. Gradually at first, and under the same conditions, portraiture develops and serves first in the identification of the individual - above all for the identification of the representatively criminal - but later also for the representatively personal. The photographic image as a document of traits in the landscape or in the person; as the historically attested witness of that which has been real, just like this and not otherwise, at the instant of the exposure. Photography becomes the silent stand-in for whoever has seen the reproduced situation in person and with his or her own eyes.

Over the course of several years, Doris Frohnapfel has sought out from all over Europe hundreds of places and regions that mark the borders between states. Out of the situations that were to be found, she has made photographs and thereby captured in an image the difference in the frontier lines. There are completely different places to be seen, naturally. Sometimes they become clearly recognisable as a border station from the border patrols or queues of trucks, although sometimes, they also seem something like a more or less charming landscape shot, when the photographer's gaze wanders over a river, a meadow or a sea. Customs controls, barbed wire fences, barriers, concrete walls, rocks, straits, people waiting with bulging plastic bags, police officers, farmland, caravans, coffee machines – Frohnapfel's subjects encompass not only the road from Gibraltar to the Bosporus, the Baltic States to North Africa, but also connect both natural and artificially made frontier lines. In part, people are to be seen, in part, functional architecture, sometimes concrete deserts, sometimes the barren waste of a no man's land. The assembled image material is heterogeneous, unspectacular and scarcely narrative. The link between the individual photographs would hardly become accessible to the viewer at all were it not for the fact that the artist provides her topography of European borders with precise indications of place and

rein dokumentarischen Charakter hatte. Erst allmählich entwickelt sich unter denselben Vorzeichen die Porträtaufnahme, die zunächst vor allem der kriminalistischen, später auch der persönlich-repräsentativen Identifizierung des Individuums dient. Das photographische Bild als Dokument landschaftlicher oder personeller Züge, als historisch verbrieftes Zeugnis dessen, was so und nicht anders im Augenblick der Aufnahme wirklich gewesen ist. Die Photographie wird zum stummen Stellvertreter desjenigen, der die abgelichtete Situation leibhaftig und mit eigenen Augen gesehen hat.

Doris Frohnapfel hat über mehrere Jahre hinweg Hunderte von Orten und Gegenden in ganz Europa aufgesucht, die zwischenstaatliche Grenzen markieren. Von den vorgefundenen Situationen hat sie Photos gemacht und die Unterschiedlichkeit der Grenzverläufe damit im Bild festgehalten. Zu sehen sind naturgemäß völlig verschiedene Orte, die manchmal durch Grenzpatrouillen oder LKW-Schlangen eindeutig als Grenzstation erkennbar werden, manchmal aber auch wie eine mehr oder weniger reizvolle Landschaftsaufnahme anmuten, wenn der Blick der Photographin über einen Fluß, eine Wiese oder das Meer schweift. Zollkontrollen, Stacheldrahtzäune, Absperrgitter, Betonmauern, Klippen, eine Meerenge, wartende Menschen mit gefüllten Plastiktüten, Polizeibeamte, Ackerland, Wohnwagen, Kaffeeautomaten – Frohnapfels Motive umspannen nicht nur die Straße von Gibraltar bis zum Bosporus, das Baltikum bis Nordafrika, sondern verbinden auch natürliche und künstlich geschaffene Grenzverläufe. Teils sind Menschen zu sehen, teils funktionale Architektur, manchmal Betonwüsten, manchmal die Ödnis eines Niemandslandes. Das gesammelte Bildmaterial ist heterogen, unspektakulär und kaum narrativ. Die Verbindung zwischen den einzelnen Photographien würde sich dem Betrachter kaum erschließen, würde die Künstlerin ihre Topographie europäischer Grenzen nicht mit genauen Orts- und Länderangaben versehen. Auf diese Weise aber thematisch sensibilisiert, beginnen die einzel-

country. In this way, sensitised thematically however, the individual depictions begin to speak. The shots, which as a result of their objects appear to range from unwieldy to banal, and are in part sentimental or amateurishly touristic, display a documentary meta-level that allows the bundle of photographs to develop into a picture atlas of Europe.

In her 'Retour' project, the artist creates a cartography of the exterior as well as the interior borders of Europe. Through her photographic definition of the selected locations as border situations, she has in the meantime recourse to a large archive of image data, one that advances through the concrete pictorial comparison to a phenomenology of the border. But what is a border exactly, when the examination undertaken by the photographs actually demonstrates the most various manifestations imaginable? A border defines the inside and the outside, it separates one from the other. I remember that on Denmark's north coast, I was fascinated as a child by the thought that I was standing with one leg in the North Sea and at the same time with the other in the Baltic Sea and that in this way, I was bridging in person the imaginary border between the two seas simultaneously. The idea that here, there coincided what had been divided, appeared in a wondrous way to heighten the tingling sensation of the cold water on my bare legs. In actual fact, however, apart from the circumstance that bathing in the sea at this spot was strictly forbidden because of the opposing wave movements that met one other there and the therefore predictably treacherous currents that resulted, everything else was presumably just like on any other beach in Denmark. And yet an almost magical effect inhabits the place in my remembrance. The mystique of the place was nourished by the knowledge that here – and only here – did the two seas collide with one another.

The Bosporus possesses a similar genius loci. It divides or joins respectively nothing less than two continents. The flow that streams between the Black Sea and the Sea of Marmara forms an

nen Abbildungen zu sprechen. Die aufgrund ihres Gegenstandes teils spröde bis banal, teils sentimentalisch oder amateurhaft touristisch anmutenden Aufnahmen entfalten eine dokumentarische Metaebene, die das Konvolut an Photographien zu einem Bilderatlas Europas werden läßt.

Die Künstlerin kartographiert in ihrem "Retour"-Projekt die europäischen Außen- wie Innengrenzen. Durch ihre photographische Bestimmung der ausgewählten Orte als Grenzsituation kann sie mittlerweile auf ein großes Archiv an Bilddaten zurückgreifen, das im konkreten Bildvergleich zu einer Phänomenologie der Grenze avanciert. Was aber ist eine Grenze, wenn doch die Sichtung der Photographien denkbar unterschiedlichste Erscheinungsweisen zeigt? Eine Grenze definiert Innen und Außen, trennt das eine vom anderen. Ich erinnere mich, dass ich als Kind an der Nordküste Dänemarks fasziniert war von dem Gedanken, dass ich mit einem Bein in der Nordsee, gleichzeitig mit dem anderen aber in der Ostsee stand und auf diese Weise die imaginäre Grenze zwischen den Meeren gleichsam leibhaftig überbrückte. Die Idee des Zusammenfalls des Getrennten schien auf wundersame Weise das Prickeln des kalten Wassers an den nackten Beinen noch zu steigern. Tatsächlich aber war bis auf den Umstand, dass das Baden im Meer an dieser Stelle wegen der aufeinandertreffenden gegensätzlichen Wellenbewegungen und der damit zu erwartenden tückischen Strömungen strengstens verboten war, alles so wie vermutlich an jedem anderen Strand Dänemarks auch. Und doch wohnt dem Ort meiner Erinnerung eine fast magische Wirkung an. Die Mystik des Ortes speiste sich aus dem Wissen, dass hier – und nur hier – die beiden Meere aufeinanderprallten.

Einen ähnlichen Genius loci besitzt der Bosporus, der nicht weniger als zwei Kontinente voneinander trennt resp. verbindet. Der Strom zwischen Schwarzem Meer und Marmarameer bildet einen geschichtsträchtigen Grenzverlauf zwischen Orient und Okzident, ist

historically pregnant frontier line between the Orient and the Occident and is the epitome both of the separation between different cultures as well as of the exchange. Inevitably, various back views of several people that Doris Frohnapfel has photographed sitting on chairs or a bench on the bank of the Bosporus, gazing over to the Asian side of Turkey on the opposite shore, henceforward become linked with the gaze cast longingly towards the other, to what lies behind, to the unreachable. Seas or cultures that plunge into one another – in both examples, it is given geographic conditions that, as the natural form of a particular view, pre-impress, and within this, frequently reach far back in history. Nonetheless, most frontier lines are created artificially and from their landscaping, they scarcely permit themselves to be imagined as the crossing from one state into another. On the contrary, they are frequently marked out as being borders through an exchangeable and typically functional architecture of the frontier post, complete with cola machine and 24 hour shopping.

The crossing of a border into another country awakens various associations. For the most part, this is connected to entering another language area, another culture, food that is typical of the country, another currency. With the introduction of the Euro into most of what now consists of 25 European member states and the simplification of trade practices within the EU, the borders have become more permeable and many have disappeared altogether. Working, living, travelling – life within Europe has become more flexible and many people move like nomads across the continent, notwithstanding previous state borders. With the opening of the frontiers, the range of goods on offer has also become standardised to the most extensive degree. Apart from a few regional differences, the consumer finds almost everywhere the same range. Alongside the goods, it is also the same images finding mass media distribution. In economically, politically and culturally unified Europe, state borders mutate into relics from olden times, times in which, during the Cold War, whole ideologies were still opposing each

sowohl Inbegriff der Trennung wie des Austausches verschiedener Kulturen. Unweigerlich verbindet sich daher mit verschiedenen Rükkenansichten mehrerer Personen, die Doris Frohnapfel auf Stühlen oder einer Bank am Ufer des Bosporus sitzend und auf die gegenüberliegende, asiatische Seite der Türkei hinüberblickend photographiert hat, der sehnsüchtige Blick nach dem Anderen, Dahinterliegenden, Unerreichbaren. Aufeinanderstoßende Meere oder Kulturen – in beiden Beispielen sind es geographische Gegebenheiten, die als natürliche Form eine bestimmte Anschauung vorprägen und historisch darin häufig weit zurückreichen. Doch die meisten Grenzverläufe sind künstlich geschaffen und lassen landschaftlich kaum an den Übergang von einem Staat in einen anderen denken, sondern sind häufig nur durch eine austauschbare, typisch funktionale Grenzpostenarchitektur inkl. Cola-Automat und 24h-Shopping als solche gekennzeichnet.

Das Überschreiten einer Grenze in ein anderes Land weckt verschiedene Assoziationen. Meistens ist es mit dem Eintritt in einen anderen Sprachraum verbunden, eine andere Kultur, landestypisches Essen, eine andere Währung. Mit der Einführung des Euro in den meisten der mittlerweile 25 europäischen Mitgliedstaaten und der Vereinfachung der Handelsgepflogenheiten innerhalb der EU sind die Grenzen durchlässiger geworden, viele sind ganz verschwunden. Arbeiten, Wohnen, Reisen – das Leben innerhalb Europas ist flexibler geworden und mancher bewegt sich wie ein Nomade auf dem Kontinent, ungeachtet früherer Staatsgrenzen. Mit der Öffnung der Grenzen hat sich auch das Warenangebot weitestgehend vereinheitlicht. Bis auf wenige regionale Unterschiede findet der Konsument fast überall dasselbe Sortiment. Neben den Waren sind es auch dieselben Bilder, die massenmediale Verbreitung finden. Im wirtschaftlich, politisch und kulturell vereinten Europa mutieren Staatsgrenzen zu Relikten aus alter Zeit, in der sich während des “Kalten Krieges” noch ganze Ideologien in Drohgebärden gegenüberstanden. In Zeiten der Globalisierung und nach dem Ende der Natio-

other with threatening gestures. In times of globalisation and after the end of national statehood within the EU, borders between countries appear to be an anachronism, whilst on the outside borders of Europe, they however give the impression of being highly armed and contested bastions, with radar technology to use against 'boat people' and other illegal immigrants. A (selected) cultural diversity of affluent faces and regional variations is increasingly growing together into a large formation underlying clearly outlined sets of legal regularities. Europe has changed over the last few years and precisely this change is also traceable at the borders, be it through their dissolution within the interior or through a reinforcement at the EU's peripheries. And thus, as the borders get moved back peu-à-peu through the expansion of the EU, so are national frontiers always also the expression of a specific interest that is subject to historical fluctuations.

How does it feel to the touch, this abstract-invisible new great power, Europe, at the beginning of the 21st century? What with the EU constitution and the many directives and guidelines coming from Brussels, is there such a thing as a European identity? In order to picture the new Europe to herself, Doris Frohnapfel has marked out photographically the borders of many member states. On the map that she created, she measures out by means of images the way the states appear and the effects they have on the outside. And what emerges to the comparative gaze that falls between the individual shots is the fundamental constructed-ness of the borders between nations. The border as a construct that is relativised historically. Thus, the ruinous remains of concrete buildings, as much as terse wire netting fences in sections of woodland, or high security sluice gates for the massive clearing away of border crossings, or as much as the carefree horse and carts on pastureland empty of people – these bear witness to the artificiality, to the being-made-ness of a border. The frontier lines are first of all brought out by the course of history and precipitated by the same – as times and interests change. The his-

nalstaatlichkeit innerhalb der EU erscheinen Ländergrenzen wie ein Anachronismus, und wirken an den europäischen Außengrenzen doch wie hochgerüstete und umkämpfte Bollwerke: mit Radartechnik gegen "boat people" und andere illegale Einwanderer. Eine (ausgewählte) kulturelle Vielfalt mit reicher Geschichte und unterschiedlichen Regionen wächst mehr und mehr zu einer Großformation zusammen, die klar umrissenen Gesetzmäßigkeiten unterliegt. Europa hat sich in den letzten Jahren verändert und genau diese Veränderung wird auch an den Grenzen spürbar, sei es durch ihre Auflösung im Binnenland oder durch eine Verstärkung an den EU-Rändern. Und so, wie sich die Grenzen peu-a-peu durch die EU-Erweiterung verschieben, so sind Landesgrenzen immer auch Ausdruck eines spezifischen Interesses, das geschichtlichen Schwankungen unterliegt.

Wie fühlt sich Europa, diese abstrakt-unsichtbare neue Großmacht, am Anfang des 21. Jahrhunderts an? Gibt es mit der EU-Verfassung und den vielen Verordnungen und Richtlinien aus Brüssel so etwas wie eine europäische Identität? Um sich ein Bild vom neuen Europa zu machen, hat Doris Frohnapfel die Grenzen vieler Mitgliedsstaaten photographisch abgesteckt. Auf ihrer so entstandenen Landkarte vermißt sie bildlich deren Erscheinungsweise und Außenwirkung. Und das, was sich dem vergleichenden Sehen zwischen den einzelnen Aufnahmen als erstes entbirgt, ist die grundsätzliche Konstruiertheit von Ländergrenzen. Die Grenze als Konstrukt, das sich geschichtlich relativiert. So zeugen sowohl ruinöse Reste von Betonbauten wie lapidare Maschendrahtzäune in Waldstücken, sowohl Hochsicherheitsschleusen für die massenhafte Abfertigung von Grenzübergängern wie unbekümmerte Pferdefuhrwerke auf menschenleerem Weideland von der Künstlichkeit, vom Gemachtsein einer Grenze. Der Lauf der Geschichte erst bringt Grenzverläufe hervor und zeitigt dieselben – im Wechsel der Zeiten und Interessen. Die historische Relativität, die in Frohnapfels Aufnahmen spürbar wird, läßt darüber selbst die strengsten Grenzbeamten als

torical relativity that becomes traceable in Frohnapfel's photographs allows even the toughest border officials to appear downright unreal as a result. The photographer's border archaeology promotes in the space of the many hundreds of photographs the revelation of subliminal layers of sediment that make everything static seem obsolete and allow history to appear as a dynamic process. Whilst her conceptual photography of border situations also documents alterations in the landscape, Doris Frohnapfel not only returns to the original function of the medium but also consummately multiplies the status of the photograph as documentary proof of that which has really happened. Whilst what is in fact to be seen in the photograph becomes for its part the documentary proof of relativity, when the present moment of perception becomes as obvious to the viewer as the moment of the photograph being taken as having been in the past – just like simultaneously, in the contemporary figure of the photographer as well, the past (and, in principle, transcience) of state power structures is brought into the open.

The artist brings border crossings into focus and through this includes further crossings in her gaze: Crossings between near and far, restrictions and open expanse, home lands and strange lands, own experience and foreign propaganda, history and the present. In spite of all the difference, the crossings come to an agreement in their flowing borders. Perception itself also finds itself constantly in a process of transition. Just as – according to your perspective – the inner European frontier lines appear now as a centre and now as a periphery, then so is perception also dependent on the individual standpoint of the viewer. The relativity of the perception however underlies not only given conditions of place but moreover – similarly to the relativity of the frontier crossings – also goes back to the historicity of seeing itself. Seeing is moulded by patterns and conventions that are socio-culturally conditioned and cannot be regarded as separate from the time historical context and cultural climate of an epoch or region. Stepping into this are the subjective

geradezu unwirklich erscheinen. Die Grenz-Archäologie der Photographin fördert im Zwischenraum der vielen Hundert Aufnahmen unterschwellige Sedimentschichten zutage, die alles Statische obsolet und Geschichte als dynamischen Prozess erscheinen lassen. Indem sie mit ihrer konzeptuellen Photographie von Grenzsituationen auch die Veränderung von Landschaft dokumentiert, kehrt Frohnapfel nicht nur zur ursprünglichen Funktion des Mediums zurück, sondern multipliziert im Vollzug auch den Status des Photos als Beleg dessen, was wirklich gewesen ist. Das, was nämlich in den Photographien zu sehen ist, wird seinerseits zum Beleg von Relativität, wenn dem Betrachter in der Gegenwart der Wahrnehmung sowohl der Moment der Aufnahme als vergangener offenbar wird, wie gleichzeitig auch in der Zeitgenossenschaft der Photographin die Vergangenheit (und prinzipielle Vergänglichkeit) von staatlichen Machtstrukturen zutage tritt.

Die Künstlerin fokussiert Grenzübergänge und hat auf diese Weise weitere Übergänge mit im Blick: Übergänge zwischen Nähe und Ferne, Begrenzung und Weite, Heimat und Fremde, eigener Erfahrung und fremder Propaganda, Geschichte und Gegenwart. Trotz aller Unterschiedlichkeit kommen die Übergänge überein in ihren fließenden Grenzen. Auch die Wahrnehmung selbst befindet sich ständig im Übergang. So wie die innereuropäischen Grenzverläufe – je nach Perspektive – mal als Zentrum, mal als Peripherie erscheinen, so ist auch die Wahrnehmung abhängig vom individuellen Betrachterstandpunkt. Die Relativität der Wahrnehmung jedoch unterliegt nicht nur örtlichen Gegebenheiten, sondern geht – ähnlich der Relativität der Grenzverläufe – auch auf die Geschichtlichkeit des Sehens selbst zurück. Das Sehen wird geprägt von Mustern und Konventionen, die sozio-kulturell bedingt sind, und kann nicht vom zeithistorischen Kontext und kulturellen Klima einer Epoche oder einer Region getrennt betrachtet werden. Dazu treten subjektive Voraussetzungen des Individuums. Wahrnehmung ist damit notwendig in vielen Aspekten, wenn auch nie gänzlich, determiniert.

assumptions of each individual. Perception is thereby necessarily determined, if also not completely, in many aspects.

The distanced eye that Doris Frohnapfel casts onto postcards that were sent back to the home country as a holiday greeting in the 1960s and 70s, by both West and East Germans, brings these borders of perception – but also simultaneously their shifting – to our attention. The artist acquired the picture postcards in second-hand shops and weaves them into her 'Retour' project as documentary material. In doing so, she proceeds in a manner similar to how she made her shots of European borders. With the greatest possible objectivity and with a distance towards sometimes emotionally charged themes in the images, she selects the settings to focus on. Both sender and recipient of these typically touristically-bound subjects remain strangers, despite knowledge of their names and addresses. The obligatory greeting to Auntie sent from holiday appears much more like an interchangeable phrase. And nevertheless the kitschy postcards speak volumes from both sides of the divided country. Sent as extremely private, and even within the autobiographical context, as scarcely meaningful communications, today they turn out to be historical witnesses from the time before the fall of the wall that led to German reunification in 1989-90, forming the end of a border regime whose wall had cost many lives. Both West and East Germans make similar choices of characteristic subjects from the time spent on holiday or the particular vacation destination (sunsets, the Eiffel Tower, Karlsplatz etc.) that are all produced for use on a massive scale and who vary at best in their print quality. In the immediate legibility of its pictorial subject, the holiday postcard fulfils no other purpose than the ascertainment of the out of the everyday routine that is associated with vacations – for the addressee and sender equally. It is the out-of-the-ordinary that is, astonishingly enough, what is mediated through the selection of a stereotypical pictorial theme, one that updates the cliché and emphasizes precisely not the uniquely individual – the picture post-

Aufmerksam auf diese Grenzen der Wahrnehmung – aber gleichzeitig auch auf deren Verschiebung – macht Doris Frohnapfels distanzierter Blick auf Postkarten, die in den 60er und 70er Jahren von West- wie Ostdeutschen als Urlaubsgrüße in die Heimat verschickt worden sind. Die Künstlerin hat die Ansichtskarten in Second-hand-Läden erworben und flicht sie als dokumentarisches Bildmaterial ein in ihr "Retour"-Projekt. Dabei geht sie ähnlich vor wie bei ihren Aufnahmen europäischer Grenzen: mit größtmöglicher Objektivität und mit Abstand zum manchmal emotional aufgeladenen Bildmotiv wählt sie die Einstellungen aus. Die Absender wie Adressaten der typisch touristisch gehaltenen Motive bleiben trotz Kenntnis der Namen und Adressen fremd, der obligatorische Gruß an die Tante aus dem Urlaub erscheint vielmehr als austauschbare Phrase. Und dennoch sprechen die kitschigen Postkarten aus beiden Teilen des geteilten Landes Bände: verschickt als überaus private und selbst im autobiographischen Kontext doch kaum bedeutungsvolle Mitteilung, geraten sie heute zum historischen Zeugnis aus der Zeit vor dem Mauerfall, der 1989/90 zur deutschen Wiedervereinigung führte und das Ende eines Grenz-Regimes mit vielen Mauer-Toten bildet. So wählen Westdeutsche wie Ostdeutsche ähnliche, die Ferienzeit oder den jeweiligen Urlaubsort charakterisierende Motive (Sonnenuntergang, Eiffelturm, Karlsplatz etc), die sämtlich für den massenhaften Gebrauch produziert worden sind und sich bestenfalls in der Druckqualität unterscheiden. Die Urlaubspostkarte erfüllt in der sofortigen Lesbarkeit des Bildmotivs keinen anderen Zweck als die Vergewisserung des urlaubsbedingt Außeralltäglichen – für den Adressaten wie Absender gleichermaßen. Vermittelt wird das Außergewöhnliche erstaunlicherweise durch die Wahl eines stereotypen Bildmotivs, das das Klischée fortschreibt und gerade nicht auf das Individuell-Einmalige abhebt – die Ansichtskarte eher als Ansicht von Sehnsüchten denn von Realität. Sie bildet einen Stellvertreter der gelebten Erfahrung, ist Folie der eigenen Projektion. Die Bildwirkung vorgefertigter Touristenmotive spricht ein unbe-

card as a picture view of longings rather than reality. It forms a stand-in for lived experience and becomes the screen for its own projection. The pictorial effect produced by pre-fabricated tourist subjects appeals to an unconscious but (inter) cultural image memory that in this connection elicits intuitively positive feelings or a calculated amazement at the distance involved. It is only when observed from a lengthy distance of time that the alteration in this intersubjective image memory shows itself. That is namely when the picture postcards from the 1960s and 70s no longer reproduce a certain wanderlust for today's viewer, but simply provoke an astonishment at a particular form of awareness of life and its aesthetic, which is today experienced as antiquated. Through this surprise and displeasure, identification is already thwarted in its early stages and an unbridgeable distance to the object created. The image has forfeited the effect of its emotional power and has gone from being the object of projected desires to the object of historicising observation. At an interval of 40 years hence, the supposedly individual has also turned out to be a heteronomous concoction that can now be looked at critically. Distantiation is thereby always also a sign for a shift in cultural memory, that at this point is no longer simply steering and fundamentally influencing subjective perception, but on the contrary, through the historicising process, also becomes itself the object of scrutiny.

With the experience of distance, a difference opens up between own, lived experience and the experience that Doris Frohnapfel describes as 'second-hand' experience. The latter distinguishes itself from the former first of all through the fact that what is suggested by the mediumistically mediated images (be it as postcards as well), was exactly what was not actually lived through itself, and thereby cannot be competently verified. Paul Virilio talks about the 'instrumentalisation of remembrance' through photographically reproduced images and consequently differentiates the 'instrumentalised (image) memory' from the 'mental memory'

wußtes, aber (inter-)kulturelles Bildgedächtnis an, das in diesem Zusammenhang intuitiv positive Gefühle oder ein kalkuliertes Staunen über das Ferne hervorruft. Erst aus einem längeren zeitlichen Abstand betrachtet, zeigt sich die Veränderung dieses intersubjektiven Bildgedächtnisses. Dann nämlich, wenn die Ansichtskarten der 60er und 70er Jahre für den heutigen Betrachter nicht länger ein gewisses Fernweh reproduzieren, sondern lediglich eine Verwunderung über eine bestimmte Form des Lebensgefühls und der Ästhetik hervorrufen, die heute als antiquiert erfahren wird. Durch dieses Befremden ist eine Identifizierung bereits im Ansatz vereitelt und eine unüberbrückbare Distanz zum Gegenstand entstanden. Das Bild hat seine emotionale Wirkmacht eingebüßt und ist vom Objekt projektiver Wünsche zum Objekt historisierender Betrachtung geworden. Im Abstand von 40 Jahren hat sich das vermeintlich Individuelle damit auch als fremdbestimmtes Machwerk entpuppt, das sich nun kritisch betrachten läßt. Distanzierung ist damit immer auch ein Indiz für eine Verlagerung des kulturellen Gedächtnisses, das die subjektive Wahrnehmung an dieser Stelle nicht länger nur unbewußt steuert und grundlegend beeinflußt, sondern das im Historisierungsprozeß plötzlich auch selbst zum Gegenstand der Betrachtung wird.

Mit der Erfahrung von Distanz tut sich eine Differenz auf zwischen der eigenen, gelebten Erfahrung und derjenigen, die Doris Frohnapfel als "second hand"-Erfahrung bezeichnet. Die letztere unterscheidet sich von der ersten dadurch, dass das, was von den medial vermittelten Bildern (und sei es als Postkarte) suggeriert wird, eben nicht selbst durchlebt wurde und es damit auch zuständlich nicht verifiziert werden kann. Paul Virilio spricht von der "Instrumentalisierung der Erinnerung" durch photographisch reproduzierte Bilder und unterscheidet demzufolge das "instrumentalisierte (Bild-)Gedächtnis" vom "mentalen Gedächtnis", dem Bilder des eigenen Vorstellungsvermögens zugrundeliegen. Ferner konstatiert er eine zunehmende Vereinnahmung der men-

which is the basis for the images' own imaginative ability. Furthermore, he detects an increasing monopoly on mental interior perception by mechanically generated images that stream over us from the outside every single day. With her border project however, Doris Frohnapfel treads a path that aims at primary experience precisely by use of the medium of photography. Taking photographs does not stand for her in the context of the accumulation of yet more secondary experience, but rather possesses in its execution the status of a reflexive inspection of information that is mediumistically mediated. In the preparation for 'Retour', she collected information on the changes taking place within Europe from various European newspapers and the Internet. With her camera in her baggage, she sought out for herself the many different border crossings that she had previously read about and literally made a picture for herself on the spot, instead of simply following a media transmitted image of things. The resulting series of photographs is therefore a documentation of her own experience as much as it is of the objective facticity of the frontier lines at the moment of the exposure being made. The depictions are not situated like the postcards in the context of the accumulation and distribution of pre-fabricated, manipulative ways of seeing, but rather form an inventory of images in which private histories as well as public ones are brought into equation with each other. Next to the unavoidable, unconscious visual memory, through her taking of photographs, Doris Frohnapfel positions an image archive that enables an immediate comparison between an image of opinion and a factual image, when she documentarily opposes the totality of an instrumentalised exterior view with her own. Her photos become thereby a catalyst for reflection before they themselves very possibly cross over into the image memory. The deviations and interfaces between the individual and the societal image archive, between mental memory and instrumentalised remembrance pull down with them the corner points of a critical search movement: Transit zones of perception on the map of political iconography.

talen Innensicht durch technisch erzeugte Bilder, die von außen Tag für Tag auf uns einströmen. Doris Frohnapfel beschreitet mit ihrem Grenz-Projekt jedoch einen Weg, der gerade mit dem Medium Photographie auf die Primärerfahrung zielt. Das Photographieren steht für sie nicht im Kontext der Anhäufung weiterer Sekundärerfahrung, sondern besitzt im Vollzug den Status reflexiven Überprüfens medial vermittelter Information. In der Vorbereitung von "Retour" hat sie aus verschiedenen europäischen Zeitungen und aus dem Internet Informationen über die Veränderungen innerhalb Europas gesammelt. Mit ihrer Kamera im Gepäck hat sie die zahlreichen verschiedenen Grenzübergänge, über die sie zuvor gelesen hat, selbst aufgesucht und sich vor Ort buchstäblich selbst ein Bild gemacht statt nur einem medienvermittelten Bild von den Dingen zu folgen. Die entstandene Photoreihe ist demnach eine Dokumentation sowohl der eigenen Erfahrung, wie auch der objektiven Faktizität dieser Grenzverläufe zum Zeitpunkt der Aufnahme. Die Abbildungen stehen nicht wie die Postkarten im Kontext der Anhäufung und Verbreitung vorfabrizierter, manipulativer Sichtweisen, sondern bilden ein Bildinventar, in dem die private wie die öffentliche Geschichte zur Gleichung gebracht werden. Doris Frohnapfel stellt mit ihren Photographien neben das unvermeidbar unbewußte visuelle Gedächtnis ein Bildarchiv, das einen unmittelbaren Vergleich zwischen Meinungsbild und faktischem Bild ermöglicht, wenn sie der Totalität einer instrumentalisierten Außensicht ihre eigene Sicht dokumentarisch gegenüberstellt. Ihre Photos werden damit zu einem Katalysator von Reflexion, bevor sie möglicherweise selbst ins Bildgedächtnis übergehen. Die Abweichungen und Schnittstellen zwischen dem individuellen und dem gesellschaftlichen Bildarchiv, zwischen mentalem Gedächtnis und instrumentalisierter Erinnerung umreißen dabei die Eckpunkte einer kritischen Suchbewegung: Transitzonen der Wahrnehmung auf der Landkarte der politischen Ikonographie.

Ulli Seegers

Car park at the border crossing point Raja Jooseppi (FIN), 29.4.2003

Outside Kirkenes airport (N), 28.4.2003

Border hills near Tårnet (N), 2.5.2003

Norwegian border crossing point to Russia, 2.5.2003

Souvenir shop Norwegian side of border crossing to Russia, 2.5.2003

Norwegian border crossing to Russia, 2.5.2003

Car park at the Norwegian border crossing point to Russia, Bus to Murmansk (RUS), 2.5.2003

Norwegian-Russian border area at Grense Jakobselv (N), 3.5.2003

Inari Lake near Virtaniemi (FIN), 29.4.2003

Woodpile in the border region of Suorsapää (FIN), 30.4.2003

Border region of Suorsapää (FIN), 30.4.2003

Inari Lake near Kessijärvi (FIN), 29.4.2003

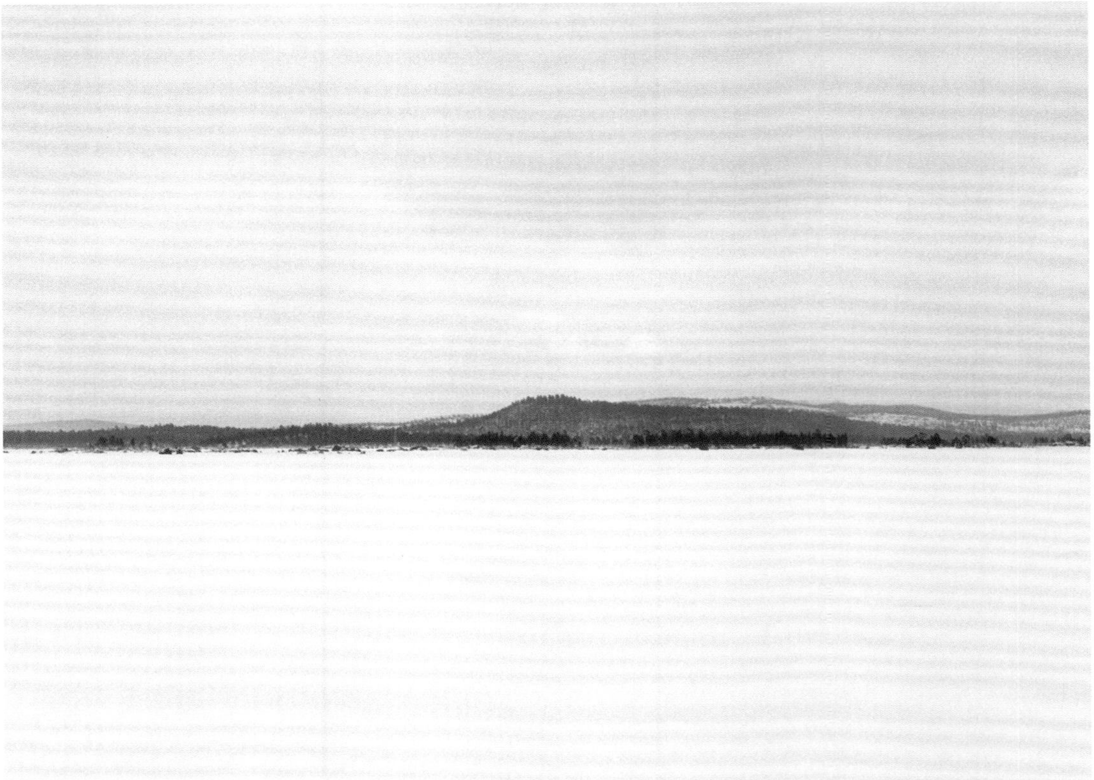

Tires on the car park at the border crossing point Raja Jooseppi (FIN), 29.4.2003

Old car, fridge etc. on the car park at Raja Jooseppi (FIN), 29.4.2003

Forest and demarcation fence in the border area of Saariselkä (FIN), 30.4.2003

Finnish-Russian border checkpoint Raja Jooseppi (FIN), 29.4.2003

Forest and demarcation fence in the border area of Saariselkä (FIN), 30.4.2003

Truck entering the ferry terminal, Bergen (N), 21.9.2004

Fence under construction at ferry terminal, Bergen (N), 21.9.2004

New fence erected after the Schengen Agreement at the ferry terminal, Bergen (N), 21.9.2004

Recently fenced entrance of Bergen ferry terminal (N), 21.9.2004

Part of monument for Lauluväljak at Tallinn Bay (EW), 5.8 2003

Sillamäe in North Estonia at the Finnish Sea (EW), 6.8.2003

Border terrain with high cliffs near Laaga at Narva Bay (EW), 6.8.2003

Via Baltica at Latvian-Estonian border, 14.8.2003

Forest in border area near Vilaka (LT), 6.8.2003

Little harbour in Mustvee at Peipsi Lake (EW), 6.8.2003

In the middle of Peipsi Lake is the Estonian-Russian border, Kallaste (EW), 6.8.2003

Stop sign on the Estonian-Latvian border, Valga/Valka, 7.8.2003

Border checkpoint for pedestrians, Valga/Valka (EW), 7.8.2003

Estonian-Latvian border fence dividing the village of Valga/Valka, 7.8.2003

Pedestrians at the border checkpoint Valga/Valka (EW), 7.8.2003

Pedestrians at the border checkpoint Valga/Valka (EW), 7.8.2003

Old military observation platform in Korti at the Via Baltica, Riga Bay (LV), 12.8.2003

Sunset at the Baltic Sea, vapour trails of international air traffic, Vitrupe (LV) 13.8.2003

Pine trees and path to the beach of the Baltic Sea near Svetciens (LV), 13.8.2003

People with rubber dinghies coming back from fishing in the Baltic Sea, Kurmrags (LV), 13.8.2003

City sign on the highway coming from Salaspils, Riga (LV), 8.8.2003

The clapped-out oil-tanker "Prestige" came from here, Ventspils harbour (LV), 9.8.2003

Ship entering Ventspils harbour, Baltic Sea (LV), 9.8.2003

Sunset at Baltic Sea, Dzeni (LT), 12.8.2003

Sunset at Baltic Sea, Sventoji (LT), 9.8.2003

Ferry from Klaipeda to Neringa (LT), 11.8.2003

The Dune at Nida (LT), 11.8.2003

Observation platform on the top of the dune near Pervalka (LT), 11.8.2003

Old military observation stand at Priel, looking North-West, (LT), 11.8.2003

Van selling roast fish on the beach, Palanga (LT), 9.8.2003

Temporary bar on the beach at the Baltic Sea, Sventoji (LT), 9.8.2003

Road E 272 near Plunge (LT), 11.8.2003

Ferry coming from Neringa, Kleipeda (LT), 11.8.2003

Border crossing point to Kaliningrad near Nida (LT), 11.8.2003

Soviet star on the obelisk at the old town-wall, Kostrzyn (PL), 7.3.2004

Border crossing point, the Polish side, Kostrzyn (PL), 7.3.2004

Border crossing point after the bridge over the Oder, Kostrzyn (PL), 7.3.2004

Border river the Oder near Kostrzyn (PL), 7.3.2004

Bridges over the Oder at Kostrzyn (PL), 7.3.2004

Boundary-post on the Oder embankment near Nw. Lubusz (PL), 7.3.2004

Polish boundary-post at the Oder near Kostrzyn (PL), 7.3.2004

Bridge from Slubice to Frankfurt/Oder (PL), 7.3.2004

Frankfurt/Oder seen from Slubice (PL), 7.3.2004

Sun-bather at the Oder in Aurith (D), 18.7.2004

Old ferry landing places between Urad (PL) and Aurith (D), 18.7.2004

Border police boat at the Oder in Eisenhüttenstadt (D), 18.7.2004

Oder meadows and flood area near Ernst Thälmann Siedlung (D), 18.7.2004

The Oder at Eisenhüttenstadt (D), 18.7.2004

Polish and German border police cars at Eisenhüttenstadt (D), 18.7.2004

German boundary-post in Coschen at the Neiße (D), 18.7.2004

German boundary-post in Sacro, on the ruins of a bridge over the Neiße (D), 19.7.2004

Polish border checkpoint, Gubin/Guben, 18.7.2004

German border checkpoint, Guben/Gubin, 18.7.2004

At the bank of the river Neiße, Coschen (D), 18.7.2004

Boundary-post on Polish bank of the Neiße, Sacro (D), 19.7.2004

Bridge over the Neiße, Guben/Gubin (D), 18.7.2004

Border crossing point, Klein Bademeusel (D), 19.7.2004

Bridge destroyed at the end of World War II, Forst (D), 19.7.2004

Ruins of the destroyed bridge, Forst (D), 19.7.2004

New construction of the border checkpoint Bad Muskau and the bridge over the Neiße (D), 19.7.2004

Bazaar on the other side of the bridge from Bad Muskau, Leknica (PL), 19.7.2004

Border crossing point, Deschka (D), 19.7.2004

Border crossing point, seen from Hirschfelde (D), 19.7.2004

New bridge over the Neiße, Görlitz-Zgorzelec (D), 19.7.2004

Border crossing point, seen from Bogatynia (PL), 19.7.2004

Border crossing point, Hagenwerder-Radomierzyce (D), 19.7.2004

Border traffic in Zgorzelec (PL), 19.7.2004

Border crossing point "Friedensstraße", Zittau-Porajow (D), 19.7.2004

On the old bridge between Görlitz and Zgorzelec (D), 19.7.2004

Entrance to the Bazaar behind the German border to Czechia, Ebersbach (D), 20.7.2004

German border seen from inside the Bazaar, (CZ), 20.7.2004

German-Czech border crossing point, Sebnitz (D), 20.7.2004

Czech-German border crossing point, Dolni Poustevna (CZ), 20.7.2004

Land surveyors preparing for new construction of the Schengen border, Terespol (PL), 13.4.2004

Land surveyors with theodolite, Terespol (PL), 13.4.2004

Women and cars waiting at the border crossing point, Terespol (PL), 13.4.2004

Construction site at the border crossing point, Terespol (PL), 13.4.2004

Bus approaching the border crossing point, Terespol (PL), 13.4.2004

Car park at the border crossing point, Terespol (PL), 13.4.2004

Shop at the car park at the border crossing point, Terespol (PL), 13.4.2004

Women waiting at the border crossing point, Terespol (PL), 13.4.2004

Bus coming from the border crossing point to Belarus, Terespol (PL), 13.4.2004

Bus and car waiting at the border crossing point, Terespol (PL), 13.4.2004

Beside of the border crossing point, Terespol (PL), 13.4.2004

Approaching the border crossing point to Ukraine, Sławatycze (PL), 13.4.2004

Polish-Ukrainian border, the river Bug at Wlodawa (PL), 14.4.2004

Polish border sign at the river Bug, Wlodawa (PL), 14.4.2004

New building for the border police, Wola Uhrushka (PL),14.4 2004

The river Bug at Wola Uhrushka (PL), 14.4.2004

Polish-Ukrainian border landscape, Okopy (PL), 14.4.2004

Parking place and construction site at the border crossing point, Okopy (PL), 14.4.2004

Car carriers waiting on the road to the border crossing point, Okopy (PL), 14.4.2004

Polish-Ukrainian border landscape, Okopy (PL), 14.4.2004

Border crossing point and bridge, Zosin (PL), 14.4.2004

Via Intermare between the Black Sea and the Baltic Sea near Hrebenne (PL), 15.4.2004

Polish and Ukrainian boundary-post, Budomierz (PL), 15.4.2004

Border crossing point to Rava Russkaja in Ukraine, Hrebenne (PL), 15.4.2004

Old synagogue, today the Museum of Jewish heritage, Wlodawa (PL), 13.4.2004

Memorial for the extermination camp Belzec, under construction, Belzec (PL), 16.4.2004

Polish post office in a former synagogue, Lubaczow (PL), 17.4.2004

Old synagogue, Skolin (PL), 17.4.2004

Polish-Ukrainian border terrain, Skolin (PL), 17.4.2004

Car park next to the border crossing point, Medyka (PL), 17.4. 2004

Construction site at the border crossing point, Medyka (PL), 17.4.2004

Men at the border crossing point, Medyka (PL), 17.4.2004

Trucks waiting on the road to Lvov for the Polish border crossing, Krakovec (PL), 17.4.2004

Truck drivers on the road to Lvov for the Polish border crossing, Krakovec (PL), 17.4.2004

Bus stop on the road to Lvov for the Polish border crossing, Krakovec (PL), 17.4.2004

Road to Lvov, Krakovec (PL), 17.4.2004

Polish-Ukrainian border crossing point in the mountains, Ustrzyki Dolne (PL), 17.4.2004

Ferry boat landing place and parking lot at the Danube near Rousse (BG), 12.10.2004

Ferry for trucks at the Danube near Rousse (BG), 12.10.2004

Border checkpoint at the ferry boat landing place near Rousse (BG), 12.10.2004

The Danube at Ryahovo (BG), 12.10.2004

Monument for a border police speedboat at the Danube, Toutrakan (BG), 12.10.2004

Black Sea at Primorsko (BG), 8.10.2004

Little lighthouse in the Black Sea at Ahtopol (BG), 8.10.2004

Benches in a park in front of an old watchtower at the Black Sea, Tsarevo (BG), 8.10.2004

The Black Sea at Dyuni (BG), 8.10.2004

Street sign near Sinemorets on the river Veleka (BG), 8.10.2004

Bulgarian flag in a private garden, Rezovo (BG), 8.10.2004

Bulgarian-Turkish border signs at the banks of the river Rezovska, Rezovo (BG), 8.10.2004

Old military surveillance path and watchtower, Rezovo (BG), 8.10.2004

Watchtower at the Black Sea, Rezovo (BG), 8.10.2004

Border fence near Malko Tarnovo (BG), 9.10.2004

Crossroad to Turkey before the Gradishte mountains, Malko Tarnovo (BG), 9.10.2004

Old border police station on the road to the border crossing point to Turkey, 9.10.2004

My rental-car on the road to the border crossing point to Turkey, near Malko Tarnovo 9.10.2004

Border crossing checkpoint at Bulgarian-Turkish border, Gradishte mountains (BG), 9.10.2004

In the middle of the border checkpoint Bulgaria-Turkey, Gradishte mountains (BG), 9.10.2004

Turkish side of the border checkpoint, Gradishte mountains (BG), 9.10.2004

Leaving the border checkpoint towards Turkey, Gradishte mountains (BG), 9.10.2004

Transmitter mast at the Bulgarian-Turkish border checkpoint, Gradishte mountains (BG), 9.10.2004

Fenced Bulgarian border strip to Turkey near Malko Tarnovo (BG), 9.10.2004

Fenced Bulgarian border strip to Turkey near Malko Tarnovo (BG), 9.10.2004

Fenced Bulgarian border strip to Turkey near Malko Tarnovo (BG), 9.10.2004

Sign at the border area near Brashlyan (BG), 9.10.2004

Fenced-in military zone at the Black Sea, Sozopol (BG), 10.10.2004

Car park at military harbour, Sozopol (BG), 10.10.2004

Close-up of military harbour, Sozopol (BG), 10.10.2004

Young man sitting on a bench at the Bosporus, Bebek (TR), 15.10.2003

Ferry crossing the Bosporus from Üsküdar to Kabatas, Istanbul (TR), 16.10.2003

The “Bridge of Europe” over the Bosporus, view from Arnavutköy, Istanbul (TR), 15.10.2003

People under an umbrella in a café next to the mosque Dolmabahce, Istanbul (TR), 16.10.2003

European bank of Istanbul at the Bosporus (TR), 15.10.2003

Boats and ship on the Bosporus, Bebek (TR), 15.10.2003

The Bosporus seen from the ferry boat, view to the "Bridge of Europe", Istanbul (TR), 19.10.2003

Bosporus and a ship-wreck seen from the Sea of Marmara, Istanbul (TR), 15.10.2003

The mosque Nusretiye at the Bosporus, seen from Sarnatkarlar Caddesi, Istanbul (TR), 15.10.2003

The Bosporus seen from above Harem Iskelesi, Istanbul (TR), 18.10.2003

The Bosporus and Beyoglu seen from Salacak Iskelesi, Istanbul (TR), 18.10.2003

Two young men waiting at Sirkeci Iskelesi, Istanbul (TR), 18.10.2003

Ferry boat from Sirkeci Iskelesi to Harem Iskelesi, Istanbul, 18.10.2003

The Bosporus at the Black Sea, 19.10.2003

Tourists at Andolu Kavagi, the "Anatolian Castle" at the Bosporus and the Black Sea (TR), 19.10.2003

The Bosporus and the Black Sea seen from Anadolu Kavagi (TR), 19.10.2003

Looking over to the European bank of the Bosporus and the Black Sea, (TR), 19.10.2003

Military harbour, Taranto (I), 1.6.2005

Ferry terminal with ferry boat to Albania, Bari (I), 1.6.2005

Strait of Otranto, view to Albania, late afternoon, Otranto (I), 1.6.2005

Strait of Gibraltar, view to Africa, early in the morning, near Tarifa (E), 29.12.2003

Security officer on the gangway to the ferry boat, Algeciras (E), 29.12.2003

Barred and glazed gangway to the ferry boat, Algeciras (E), 29.12.2003

The gangway to the ferry boat, Algeciras (E), 29.12.2003

Passengers on the gangway to the ferry boat, Algeciras (E), 29.12.2003

Passengers Terminal, Algeciras (E), 29.12.2003

The harbour seen from the parking lot, Algeciras (E), 29.12.2003

Security check in the harbour, Algeciras (E), 29.12.2003

Waiting hall for the security check in the harbour, Algeciras (E), 29.12.2003

Family on the ferry boat crossing the Strait of Gibraltar, 29.12.2003

Road to the border crossing point to Morocco, Ceuta (E), 29.12.2003

Family playing in the city park, Ceuta (E), 29.12.2003

Border area to Morocco seen from Ceuta (E), 29.12.2003

Road to the border crossing point to Morocco, Ceuta (E), 29.12.2003

Spanish side of the border checkpoint to Morocco, Ceuta (E), 29.12.2003

Close-up of people waiting at the border checkpoint to Morocco, Ceuta (E), 29.12.2003

Fence and wall at the border checkpoint to Morocco, Ceuta (E), 29.12.2003

Man sitting and waiting at the border checkpoint to Morocco, Ceuta (E), 29.12.2003

New harbour building next to the old castle, Tarifa (E), 31.12.2003

Ferry to Tanger in the harbour of Tarifa, seen from the old castle (E), 31.12.2003

Passport control at the ferry terminal, Tarifa (E), 31.12.2003

Door of the border checkpoint, Gibraltar (GB), 30.12.2003

Opened door of the border checkpoint, Gibraltar (GB), 30.12.2003

Family on the road to the border crossing point of Gibraltar, La Linea de la Concepción (E), 30.12.2003

Airport at the border checkpoint, Gibraltar (GB), 30.12.2003

View over the Strait of Gibraltar, Gibraltar (GB), 30.12.2004

View to Africa from the Point of Europe, Gibraltar (GB), 30.12.2003

Beach ouside Tarifa (E), 31.12.2003

Harbour, Tarifa (E), 31.12.2003

Boat at the beach outside Tarifa (E), 31.12.2003

Red cross boat in the harbour, Tarifa (E), 31.12.2003

Camper on a car park at the beach, Tarifa (E), 31.12.2003

Wind surf observation tower at the beach near Tarifa (E), 31.12.2003

Alto el Cabrito next to Tarifa (E), 31.12.2003

Bunker and camper at Punta Marroqui, Tarifa (E), 31.12.2003

Camp site next to Tarifa (E), 31.12.2003

Camp site next to Tarifa (E), 31.12.2003

Camper and lighthouse at Cabo de Trafalgar (E), 31.12.2003

Checkpoint of military zone La Rota, Cadiz (E), 1.1.2004

Close-up of military zone La Rota, Cadiz (E), 1.1.2004

War ships in the harbour of La Rota (E), 1.1.2004

Basque country side, Ondarroa (E), 5.1.2004

Gernika, Basque country (E), 5.1.2004

Toll booth on the highway E 80 near Miranda de Ebro (E), 2.1.2004

Demonstration in front of the Guggenheim Museum, Bilbo/Bilbao (E), 3.1.2004

Close-up of demonstrators' banderole, Bilbo/Bilbao (E), 3.1.2004

Sign warning of a dirty beach as a result of the shipwrecked "Prestige", Algorta (E), 4.1.2004

Bay of Vizcaya, Donostia/San Sebastian (E), 6.1.2004

Bay of Vizcaya, Hondarribia (E), 7.1.2004

Border between snow, trees and provinces, Puerto de Piqueras (E), 1710 m, 8.1.2004

Snow fence, Puerto de Piqueras (E), 1710 m, 8.1.2004

Remains of bunkers at the Strait of Calais, Wissant (F), 25.3.2005

Memorial for Bleriot and his channel crossing with a Monoplane 1909, Sangatte (F), 26.3.2005

Ferries crossing the channel, in the foreground the site of the former refugee camp,Sangatte,27.2.2002

Strait of Calais, Cap Gris Nez (F), 27.3.2005

Camper at the Strait of Calais, Cap Blanc Nez (F), 26.3.2005

Ferry terminal, Calais (F), 27.3.2005

Fence of ferry terminal, Dunkerque (F), 27.3.2005

Sign on the fence, Peuplingues (F), 28.3.2005

Fenced-in Eurostar entrance to the Channel Tunnel, Peuplingues (F), 28.3.2005

Ferry terminal, Calais (F), 27.3.2005

Eurotunnel terminal, Coquelles (F), 25.3.2005

Fenced-area containing tunnel ventilation, West, Sangatte (F), 26.3.2005

Fenced-area containing tunnel ventilation, South, Sangatte (F), 26.3.2005

Fenced-area containing tunnel ventilation device, East, Sangatte (F), 26.3.2005

Close-up of fenced-in Eurostar entrance to the Channel Tunnel, Peuplingues (F), 25.3.2005

Fenced-in Eurostar entrance to the Channel Tunnel, Peuplingues (F), 25.3.2005

Bridge with fence to the Eurostar entrance to the Channel Tunnel, Peuplingues (F), 28.3.2005

Bridge with fence to the Eurostar entrance to the Channel Tunnel, Peuplingues (F), 28.3.2005

Retour, Reportage

If asked what I am currently working on, I have always somewhat hesitantly entitled the project "Europe" - and then immediately the qualifications followed. For what does the word really express? The potential limit itself, the "borders of Europe", only brought with it new restrictions. What I planned was compiled in a fragmentary way and went back to a subjective selection. Meanwhile, "Places of Transition in Europe" seemed to me to be a suitable working title. However, since, after a few trips, I had (almost) never actually crossed the borders, but instead had always either gazed at or photographed respectively the frontiers, rivers, fences and border stations from what I called the safe 'distance of Schengen', I found myself perhaps physically in such a transitional place whilst being nevertheless precisely just as far away from it.

I have only ever been a West European in any case, have always had respect for the "Iron Curtain" and have now moreover become, as a result of the political and territorial shifts in Europe, just a "Schengen European". I did not want to use my project to define what Europe means, where it begins, where it ends, and also considered for a time the title "Europe and Turkey", in order to encapsulate that on the other hand, there are no firm borders in this case, thereby furthermore referring to an as yet unresolved and lengthy dispute over the self definition of the European Union. However, the context again appeared too narrow to me and out of this came: "Europe, Turkey and Israel". I got out my Israel photos from 1995 again. I remembered a curious occurrence at a checkpoint. We had been travelling by bike, and already directly after Jerusalem we had gone through controls on the road to the Dead Sea, then travelled downhill all the way and it was not until we were on the stretch running alongside the Dead Sea that, even from some distance away, we again caught sight of the red and white painted drums, plastic barricades and Stop signs that announced a checkpoint. The road was reduced to one lane, meaning that vehicles had

Wurde ich gefragt, woran ich gerade arbeite, habe ich das Projekt immer etwas zögernd mit "Europa" betitelt, und es folgten dann direkt die Einschränkungen, denn was sagt das Wort schon aus – selbst die mögliche Einengung, die "Grenzen Europas" brachte nur wieder neue Einschränkungen mit sich. Was ich vorhatte, war fragmentarisch angelegt und ging auf eine subjektive Auswahl zurück. Zwischendurch schien mir als Arbeitstitel "Übergangsorte in Europa" geeignet. Da ich aber, nach ein paar Reisen, die Grenzen (fast) nie tatsächlich überschritten habe, sondern immer aus sicherem, wie ich das dann nannte, "Schengen-Abstand" auf die Grenzen, die Flüsse, die Zäune, die Grenzstationen blickte, bzw. photographierte, befand ich mich vielleicht physisch in so einem Übergangsort und war doch genauso weit davon entfernt.

Ich bin ohnehin immer nur Westeuropäerin gewesen, habe immer Respekt vor dem "Eisernen Vorhang" gehabt und bin nun durch die politischen und territorialen Verschiebungen in Europa auch nur zur "Schengen-Europäerin" geworden. Ich wollte mit meinem Projekt nicht bestimmen, was Europa bedeutet, wo es anfängt, wo es endet und dachte auch eine Zeitlang an den Titel "Europa und die Türkei", um einzuschliessen, dass es andererseits in diesem Fall keine festen Grenzen gibt und nahm damit auch Bezug auf eine noch nicht ausgestandene größere Querele über die Selbstdefinition der Europäischen Union. Der Rahmen erschien mir jedoch weiterhin zu eng und daraus wurde: "Europa, Türkei und Israel". Ich holte noch einmal meine Israelphotos von 1995 heraus. Ich erinnerte mich an eine kuriose Begebenheit an einem Kontrollpunkt. Wir waren mit dem Fahrrad unterwegs und schon direkt hinter Jerusalem, auf der Strasse zum Toten Meer durch Kontrollen gekommen, dann immer bergab gefahren und erst auf der Strecke am Toten Meer entlang sah man schon von weitem wieder die rot-weiss angemalten Fässer, Plastikbarrikaden und Stop-Schilder, die einen Kontrollpunkt ankündigten. Die Straße wird auf

to travel slowly because of potential oncoming traffic. This type of checkpoint was probably mobile, for here there were erected only a tent and a wooden shack, plus a bench that could be installed underneath it, come rain or shine. On the photo that was taken then, four soldiers are standing around, more bored and relaxed than anything else – smoking cigarettes with sunglasses and machine guns – apparently free of any major statutory formalities. As had so often been the case, amazement was expressed at our bicycle tour and a few jokes were cracked – but nevertheless it was soon "back to business": "Passport!" – We showed our passports and I asked them if I could photograph them. They had nothing against it, struck a bit of a pose and carried on with their jokes. I took two photographs. The guy at the front, hands on hips, is laughing in a really friendly way into the camera, the next guy is standing somewhat awkwardly next to him and the other two are sitting casually against the back of the bench. The sun is shining and casting long shadows in the sand. We packed our passports away again, then my camera, and journeyed on. Often when I am travelling and taking photographs, there are only a very few recognisable external differences between me and a tourist. Exactly like the tourist, I am travelling in order to collect images, and these images are both objective and material like picture postcards, snapshots and videos, as well as subjective and immaterial, like hopes, dreams and visions. I also have, like many tourists, a vague idea of what it is that I am going to see, but I am still prepared time and time again to risk leaving it to the actual encounter. It was in this word, 'tourist', then, that a part of my eventual title was also to be found: the tour – and since I continually, and fairly rapidly, used to return to my point of departure, then from that was derived: Retour.

A journey also always has a border. As soon as a country to which I wanted to travel had been decided upon, then I immediately got a ticket for a return flight, hired a car upon arrival and drove for seven to ten days through regions that I had previously roughly researched. Each time, I had a digital camera with me, a laptop, a tripod

nur eine Fahrbahn reduziert, so dass Fahrzeuge wegen möglichen Gegenverkehrs langsam fahren müssen. Wahrscheinlich waren diese Art Kontrollpunkte mobil, denn hier war nur ein Zelt und eine Bretterbude mit Bank zum Unterstellen bei Regen oder Sonne aufgestellt. Auf dem Photo, das damals entstand, stehen vier Soldaten herum, eher gelangweilt und entspannt – Zigarette rauchend mit Sonnenbrillen und Maschinengewehren – scheinbar ohne große Formvorschriften. Wie so oft wunderte man sich über unsere Fahrradtour und machte sich ein bisschen lustig – aber nichts desto trotz "back to business": "Passport!?" – Wir zeigten unsere Pässe und ich fragte sie, ob ich sie photographieren könnte. Sie hatten nichts dagegen, schmissen sich ein bisschen in Pose und machten weiter ihre Scherze. Ich machte zwei Photos: der vorderste lacht, Arme in die Hüften gestützt, wirklich freundlich in die Kamera, der nächste steht etwas unbeholfen daneben, die beiden anderen sitzen lässig auf der Lehne der Bank. Die Sonne scheint und sie werfen lange Schatten im Sand. Wir packten unsere Pässe wieder ein, dann meine Kamera und fuhren weiter. Es gibt oft nur wenige erkennbare äußerliche Unterschiede zwischen mir, wenn ich reise und Fotos mache und einem Touristen. Genau wie der Tourist, reise ich, um Bilder zu sammeln und diese Bilder sind sowohl objektiv und materiell wie Ansichtskarten, Schnappschüsse und Videos, als auch subjektiv und immateriell wie Hoffnungen, Träume und Visionen. Ich habe auch, wie viele Touristen eine vage Vorstellung von dem, was ich sehen werde, lasse es aber immer wieder auf die wirkliche Begegnung ankommen. In diesem Wort, Tourist, steckte dann auch ein Teil meines endgültigen Titels: die Tour – und da ich immer wieder, einigermaßen schnell, auch zu den Ausgangspunkten zurückkehrte, wurde daraus: Retour.

Eine Reise hat immer auch eine Grenze. War die Entscheidung für ein Land, in das ich reisen wollte, gefallen, nahm ich sofort auch ein Rückflugticket, mietete vor Ort ein Auto und fuhr sieben bis zehn Tage durch vorher ungefähr recherchierte Gebiete. Ich hatte jedesmal eine Digitalkamera dabei, einen Laptop, ein Stativ,

and a Hasselblad. Evenings in the hotel, then, were always a case of transferring images from the camera onto the computer, sorting through them, and burning them onto a CD. For this reason, an important criterion when selecting a room was whether an electrical socket was available. In addition to that, a good map, one that was not too old, was indispensable.

Besides, over the past few years I have been collecting maps and statistics. The kind that assist in illustrating old and new facts about the old and new European territories. Shortly before 1 May 2004, the new "centre" of Europe was located by the National Geographic Institute in France (IGN). The geographic mid-point of all the 25 EU states is now Kleinmaischeid, with 1300 inhabitants and lying around 40 km south east of Bonn in Germany. This was calculated using the mathematical formula that produces the mid-point of a surface area when the outlines of that surface area are known. The map of Europe and the detailed maps of individual countries in my pocket diary gave me the first chance of an overview on my project. The European borders in the north, south and west lie almost exclusively on the sea, only those in the east are inland borders, and in a few years will be in part on the Black Sea. Borders occur at geographical obstacles like mountains, rivers, lakes, deserts and seas. In his chapter "Marking out boundaries" from 'The Practice of Everyday Life', de Certeau says: "In the traditional language of court proceedings, magistrates formerly 'visited the scene of the case at issue', in order to 'hear' the contradictory statements made by the parties to a dispute concerning debatable boundaries." Most borders were drawn with force. If the political consolidation did not last long, then they were (again by use of force) shifted. Through looking at the weather maps in the newspapers, my first clear – if nonetheless abstract – impression, gained from looking at the map of Europe in my pocket diary, could become blurred and was sometimes replaced by a report on the atmosphere of the weather. Once I had decided on a region that I wanted to travel to, then I looked in the Internet and bookshops for cartographic information. In

eine Hasselblad. Abends im Hotel hieß es dann stets Bilder von der Kamera auf den Computer zu überspielen, zu sortieren und auf CD zu brennen. Wichtiges Kriterium bei der Zimmersuche war deshalb, ob eine Steckdose vorhanden war. Weiterhin war eine gute, nicht zu alte, Landkarte unentbehrlich.

In den letzten Jahren habe ich im übrigen Karten und Statistiken gesammelt. Solche, die alte und neue Fakten des alten und neuen europäischen Territoriums illustrieren helfen. Kurz vor dem 1. Mai 2004 wurde das neue "Zentrum" Europas vom Nationalen Geographischen Institut in Frankreich (IGN) lokalisiert. Der geographische Mittelpunkt aller 25 EU-Staaten ist jetzt Kleinmaischeid, mit 1300 Einwohnern und liegt ca. 40 km südöstlich von Bonn in Deutschland. Dies wurde mit der mathematischen Formel, die den Mittelpunkt einer Oberfläche ergibt, wenn deren Umrisse bekannt sind, errechnet. Die Europakarte und die Länderdetailkarten in meinem Taschenkalender gaben mir den ersten Überblick über mein Projekt. Die europäischen Grenzen im Norden, Westen und Süden liegen fast ausschließlich am Meer, nur die im Osten liegen auf dem Land und in ein paar Jahren teils am Schwarzen Meer. Grenzen entstehen an geographischen Hindernissen, wie Gebirgen, Flüssen, Seen, Wüsten und Meeren. In seinem Kapitel "Grenzziehungen" meint de Certeau in "Kunst des Handelns": "Der schönen traditionellen Sprache der Gerichtsprotokolle zufolge 'begaben sich' die Richter früher an 'Ort und Stelle', um bei Grenzstreitigkeiten die widersprüchlichen Aussagen der Parteien 'anzuhören'". Die meisten Grenzen wurden gewaltsam gezogen; währte die politische Erstarrung nicht lange, wurden sie (wiederum gewaltsam) verschoben. Durch die Wetterkarten in Tageszeitungen konnte der erste klare, wenn auch abstrakte Eindruck, den ich beim Betrachten der Europakarte meines Taschenkalenders hatte, verschwimmen und wurde manchmal durch ein Wetterstimmungsbild ersetzt. Hatte ich mich dann für eine Region, in die ich reisen wollte, entschieden, suchte ich im Internet und im Buchhandel nach kartographischen Informa-

the case of Spain, I spent a long time asking myself if it were possible to achieve the following with a car in ten days: To drive from Madrid to Andalusia, there to explore the coast from Cadiz to Algeciras to Gibraltar, as well as make a detour to Ceuta over the Strait of Gibraltar, then to drive the whole way through Spain from the south to the north (1050 km) to Bilbao and San Sebastian in the Basque country and then back again to the airport past Madrid? I bought an up-to-date map, this showed all the 'new' motorways and it seemed that, without a stop in Madrid, it would be feasible.

Coming out of Madrid on the motorway, the border into the Basque country most markedly draws attention to itself in the form of a toll booth. Then it runs past high mountain ranges, through a ravine and now the road signs are in two languages. In the Atlas of Globalisation, the Spanish and French Basques are marked in orange on a graphic showing the 'conflicts and centres of tension within the EU', next to the Bretons and the Corsicans, as 'attempts towards autonomy by means of armed actions'; in differentiation to the former Yugoslavia, Cyprus and Northern Ireland, which are designated in red as 'armed conflicts'. In front of the Guggenheim museum in Bilbao, opposite the Jeff Koons "Puppy" sculpture made from pansies, demonstrators line up in a long row holding a banderole with hundreds of black and white portraits. A few people are distributing pamphlets. They are protesting against the isolation of the Basque prisoners in prisons scattered across the whole of Spain and France. They are demanding that prisoners be held together in Basque prisons, so that people can be visited more easily by their friends and relatives – several people had already lost their lives in car accidents while making such visits and the long car journeys they required. I stop here for a while and do some photographing. The people who are holding the banderole look sad, while the portraits of the detainees give off more of a normal or even cheerful impression, since they probably all originate from family albums or boxes of photos. On the coast, a sign warns against bathing, for pollutants are still to be

tionen. Für Spanien fragte ich mich lange Zeit, ob es möglich war, in zehn Tagen mit dem Auto folgendes zu schaffen: von Madrid nach Andalusien zu fahren, dort die Küste von Cadiz nach Algeciras und Gibraltar zu erkunden, sowie einen Abstecher nach Ceuta durch die Strasse von Gibraltar zu machen, dann komplett von Süden nach Norden (1050 km) durch Spanien nach Bilbao und San Sebastian ins Baskenland zu fahren und wieder zurück zum Flughafen nach Madrid? Ich kaufte eine aktuelle Landkarte, diese zeigte alle "neuen" Autobahnen und es erschien ohne Aufenthalt in Madrid durchführbar.

Aus Madrid über die Autobahn kommend macht sich die Grenze zum Baskenland vor allem in Form einer Mautstelle bemerkbar. Es geht dann, an hohem Gebirge vorbei, durch eine Schlucht und die Schilder sind nun zweisprachig. Die spanischen und französichen Basken sind im Atlas der Globalisierung auf einer Graphik, die die "Konflikte und Spannungsherde innerhalb der EU" zeigt, in Orange neben den Bretonen und Korsen als "Autonomiebestrebungen mit bewaffneten Aktionen" verzeichnet; in Abgrenzung zu Ex-Jugoslawien, Zypern und Nordirland, die in Rot als "Bewaffnete Konflikte" bezeichnet werden. Vor dem Guggenheimmuseum in Bilbao, gegenüber der Stiefmütterchenskulptur "Puppy" von Jeff Koons, stehen in einer langen Reihe Demonstrierende, eine Banderole mit hunderten von schwarz-weißen Portraits haltend. Ein paar Leute verteilen Flugblätter. Sie protestieren gegen die Vereinzelung der baskischen Gefangenen in Gefängnisse verstreut über ganz Spanien und Frankreich. Sie fordern eine Zusammenlegung in baskische Gefängnisse, so dass die Leute von Ihren Freunden und Verwandten einfacher besucht werden können; es wären auch schon einige Personen auf solchen Besuchen und den damit verbundenen langen Autofahrten bei Autounfällen ums Leben gekommen. Hier bleibe ich ein bißchen stehen und photographiere. Die Menschen, die die Banderole halten, sehen traurig aus, die Portraits der Inhaftierten wirken eher normal oder sogar fröhlich, weil sie wohl alle aus Familienalben und Photokartons stammen. An

encountered as a result of the accident that befell the 'Prestige' in 2002. This clapped-out oil-tanker came from Ventspils, the port in Latvia through which Russia ships raw materials and which I had already visited the previous summer. On the return journey to Madrid I take another route and on this one, my border experience lies at 1710 metres, at Puerto de Piqueras, which is simultaneously the regional border to Castilla Y Léon – a frontier of snow and trees.

The map of Europe in my pocket diary shows the furthest points that I visited and photographed: Kirkenes in the north and Ceuta and Istanbul in the south.

The North is vast and lonely. In Finland it took me five hours to do 200 km because it suddenly began to snow at the end of April and in a short time, 20 cm of snow were lying on the isolated country road. In Raja-Jooseppi, one of the most northerly frontier stations between Finland and Russia, I first asked the Finns and then the Russians if it would be possible to obtain a day's visa to travel into Russia. The former referred me to the latter, who in their turn did not understand my question. There was no way through here. Quite different to the border between Finland and Norway, in Utsjoki, on the same tour. Here I crossed the border without noticing it. When I did notice it, shortly after the bridge, I didn't deem it necessary to stop and take a photo. It had been raining cats and dogs for some time in any case.

The East is defined through post-Communistic conditions and circumstances. The Baltic States have re-installed their state borders for the first time since their independence. On the ten-day tour through Estonia, Latvia and Lithuania, we cross these four times. And for the Russian enclave Kaliningrad, we would again have had to apply for a visa months earlier. In Valka, a village lying on the border between Estonia and Latvia, a small queue of cars formed on either side, because the cars – the passports too, naturally – but particularly the cars were being checked over. Papers, engine number, boot, hub caps etc. There were two Range Rovers opposite me. I saw the Italian number-plates and asked

der Küste warnt ein Schild vor dem Baden, denn es sind immer noch Verunreinigungen durch die Havarie der "Prestige" im Jahre 2002 zu erwarten. Dieser marode Öltanker kam aus Ventspils, dem Hafen in Lettland, über den Rußland Rohstoffe verschifft und den ich bereits im Sommer zuvor besucht hatte. Auf der Rückreise nach Madrid nehme ich eine andere Strecke und auf dieser liegt meine Grenzerfahrung auf 1710 Metern, dem Puerto de Piqueras, gleichzeitig auch die Regionalgrenze zu Castilla Y León – eine Baum- und Schneegrenze.

Die Europakarte meines Taschenkalenders zeigt die äußersten Punkte die ich besuchte und photographierte: im Norden Kirkenes und im Süden Ceuta und Istanbul.

Der Norden ist weit und einsam. In Finnland brauchte ich für 200 km fünf Stunden, weil es plötzlich Ende April anfing zu schneien und nach kurzer Zeit lagen 20 cm Schnee auf der abgeschiedenen Landstrasse. In Raja-Jooseppi, einer der nördlichsten Grenzstationen zwischen Finnland und Russland, fragte ich erst die Finnen, dann die Russen, ob es möglich sei ein Tagesvisum nach Russland zu bekommen. Erstere verwiesen mich an letztere, die wiederum meine Frage nicht verstanden. Hier war kein Durchkommen. Ganz anders auf der gleichen Tour an der Grenze zwischen Finnland und Norwegen in Utsjoki. Hier bin ich über die Grenze gefahren, ohne dass es mir auffiel. Als ich das kurz hinter der Brücke doch merkte, hielt ich es nicht für nötig anzuhalten, um ein Photo zu machen. Es regnete auch schon seit einiger Zeit in Strömen.

Der Osten ist bestimmt durch post-kommunistische Befindlichkeiten und Umstände. Die baltischen Staaten haben nach ihrer Unabhängigkeit erstmal wieder ihre Staatsgrenzen installiert. Auf der zehntägigen Tour durch Estland, Lettland und Litauen passieren wir diese viermal. Und für die russische Enklave Kaliningrad hätten wir wieder Monate vorher ein Visum beantragen müssen. In Valka, einem Dorf das auf der Grenze von Estland und Lettland liegt, bildete sich eine kleine Autoschlange auf beiden Seite, weil die Autos,

the driver and his family in the first vehicle where they came from and a short conversation ensued. They were on holiday, they were travelling from Turin to St. Petersburg. The shorter route actually led even further down from here, through Belarus, but there were queues kilometres long at that border – and they didn't want to wait, they wanted to drive. After the car's all-over check by the Latvian border police, I get sent to the side entrance of the little frontier station, because I have to buy a Latvian insurance policy which, with an additional charge, should then also be valid for Lithuania. In Poland, at the border with Ukraine near Krakovec, I saw the longest queue of trucks. Several kilometres. One truck after another. I don't know how long they had been standing there and waiting. Definitely for a few days. The truck drivers moved around in groups, had barbecues or made coffee at the edge of road. We drove past in the car in the opposite direction and I stopped now and again to take a look. I only ever get out very briefly, in order to take a photograph.
"No press, no, no!!!" scolded or shouted some people. I was only partly intimidated – so long as it wasn't the border police. Because they always had something against me photographing the border, from whatever distance away. And they can make unnecessary trouble. Who actually knows at what distance it is forbidden to photograph a border and who would want to discuss that in a language that they didn't understand? In Kostryzn, on the border between Poland and Germany, shortly before 1 May, we got into a quarrel with the border officials over photographing from a distance of 300 metres. After 1 May, we then walked with the camera over the Oder and the Neisse, the borderline supposed to guarantee peace between Germany and Poland, and this time entirely without this sort of harassment. In any event, if police came, I always packed the camera away. In fact, what I would like is to photograph the places that I have seen. But it depends for me neither on having been very close to the sites, nor is it the situation of the actual frontier huts, nor the faces of the occupants that I want to photograph,

natürlich auch die Pässe, aber vor allem die Autos, durchgecheckt werden. Papiere, Motornummer, Kofferraum, Radkappen etc. Mir gegenüber standen zwei Range Rover. Ich sah die italienischen Nummernschilder und fragte den Fahrer und seine Familie des ersten Autos woher sie kommen und es entwickelte sich ein kurzes Gespräch. Sie machten Urlaub, sie fuhren von Turin nach St. Petersburg. Die kürzere Strecke führte eigentlich weiter unten durch Belarus, aber an der Grenze waren kilometerlange Schlangen; sie wollten nicht warten, sondern fahren. Nach dem Autototalcheck der lettischen Grenzpolizei schickt man mich zu dem Seiteneingang der kleinen Grenzstation, weil ich eine lettische Versicherungspolice kaufen muss, die dann mit einem Aufpreis auch für Litauen gelten sollte. In Polen an der Grenze zur Ukraine bei Krakovec habe ich die längste Lkw-Schlange gesehen. Einige Kilometer. Ein Lkw hinter dem anderen. Ich weiß nicht wie lange sie dastehen und warten, sicher ein paar Tage. Die Lkw-Fahrer liefen in Gruppen herum, grillten oder kochten Kaffee am Straßenrand. Wir fuhren mit dem Auto in entgegengesetzter Richtung daran vorbei und ich hielt ab und zu an, um zu schauen. Um Photos zu machen, steige ich immer nur kurz aus.
"No presse, no, no!!!" Keine Presse, schimpften, schrien manche. Ich war nur bedingt eingeschüchtert – solange es nicht die Grenzpolizei war. Denn die hatte immer etwas dagegen, daß ich die Grenze photographierte, egal aus welcher Entfernung. Und sie können einem unnötigen Ärger machen. Wer weiß schon, mit welchem Abstand es verboten ist, eine Grenze zu photographieren und wer möchte sowas in einer Sprache, die man nicht versteht, diskutieren. In Kostryzn an der Grenze von Deutschland nach Polen geraten wir kurz vor dem 1. Mai mit den Grenzbeamten in einen Streit über das Photographieren aus einer Entfernung von 300 Metern. Nach dem 1. Mai spazierte man dann mit dem Photoapparat über die Oder und die Neiße, die Friedensgrenze von Deutschland nach Polen, dann schon ganz ohne diese Schikanen. Jedenfalls packte ich, wenn Polizei kam, immer die Kamera weg. Ich möchte zwar die Orte

as in the two photos that I made at the Israeli checkpoint. On the Via Intermare, between the Black and the Baltic Sea near Hrebenne on the Ukrainian border, on the Polish side, I had already stopped in order to photograph the border and especially the building site to the left. If the frontier stations had not already been anyway recently built, enlarged and made safer, then they were at the very least building sites. In Terespol, the first place on the tour along the eastern border of Poland, there were land surveyors working with theodolites behind us. In Hrebenne, a jeep overtook us that braked sharply when it saw me with the camera. It stopped, turned around and came closer. Didn't speak German, didn't speak Polish...I signed to him, that I was going to pack the camera away and was just a tourist. They were satisfied with that and drove back.

The South is eventful and densely populated. The Strait of Gibraltar and the Bosporus were navigated by countless ferry links. The Bosporus, border between Europe and Asia, is an old border. Istanbul lies on both banks, on the European and on the Asiatic continent. At this border, the only people taking photographs on the pleasure steamer that travels almost all the way up to the Black Sea were the numerous tourists. There are no further controls here, to the west as well as to the east lies Turkey – European-Asiatic. On our first crossing of the Bosporus, still with the ferry, we were the only ones who lingered up on deck since it was very windy and cold. The waiter from the bar observed us and brought us a freshly squeezed orange juice in a friendly manner, mischievously congratulating us on our crossing to the other continent, only then, as we slowly moored on the other bank, to make us a sign as to how much this orange juice that we had not ordered cost. We were taken aback and amused, such great flair for business was not to be ignored, and we paid a tip. At the end of the Bosporus, on the Black Sea, there lies on the western side a European fortress, the 'European Castle' and on the eastern side, an Asiatic one – the 'Anatolian Castle'. At the border crossing in Ceuta, from Spain to Morocco, I was pelted with stones. One

photographieren, die ich gesehen habe, es kommt mir aber weder darauf an ganz nah dran gewesen zu sein, noch ist die Situation des tatsächlichen Grenzhäuschen oder die Gesichter der GrenzerInnen das, was ich photographieren will; so wie auf den beiden Photos, die ich an dem israelischen Checkpoint gemacht hatte. Auf der Via Intermare, zwischen Schwarzem und Baltischem Meer bei Hrebenne an der ukrainischen Grenze, auf polnischer Seite, hatte ich schon angehalten, um die Grenze und vor allem die Baustelle links zu photographieren. Wenn die Grenzstationen nicht sowieso schon neugebaut, vergrößert, sicherer gemacht wurden, so waren es zumindest Baustellen. In Terespol, dem ersten Ort der Tour an der polnischen Ostgrenze, waren hinter uns Vermesser mit Theodolithen an der Arbeit. In Hrebenne überholte uns ein Jeep, der scharf bremst, als er mich mit der Kamera sah. Er hielt, drehte und kam näher. Kein Deutsch, kein polnisch... ich machte ihnen Zeichen, daß ich die Kamera wegpacken werde und nur Tourist bin. Sie waren damit zufrieden und fuhren zurück.

Der Süden ist ereignisreich und stark bevölkert. Die Straße von Gibraltar und der Bosporus werden mit unzähligen Fährverbindungen befahren. Der Bosporus, die Grenze zwischen Europa und Asien ist eine alte Grenze. Istanbul liegt an beiden Ufern, auf europäischem und asiatischem Kontinent. Auf dieser Grenze waren es nur die vielen Touristen, die auf dem Ausflugsdampfer, der bis kurz vors Schwarze Meer fährt, photographierten. Hier sind keine weiteren Kontrollen, westlich wie östlich liegt die Türkei – europäisch-asiatisch. Bei der ersten Überquerung des Bosporus noch mit der Fähre waren wir die einzigen, die sich oben an Deck aufhielten, weil es sehr windig und kalt war. Die Kellner der Bar beobachteten uns und brachten uns freundlich einen frisch gepressten Orangensaft und gratulierten schelmisch zur Überfahrt zum anderen Kontinent, um dann, als wir langsam am anderen Ufer anlegten, uns Zeichen machen, wieviel der Orangensaft kostete, den wir nicht bestellt hatten. Wir waren verdutzt und erheitert, soviel Geschäftssinn will nicht ignoriert sein, und wir bezahlten mit

of my final border situations is once again going to be a touristic one – the Riviera on the Black Sea.

Le Monde Diplomatique and the Atlas of Globalisation assembled a map of Europe that made the Schengen border distinct in the form of a clear red line, and allocated on there circles large and small, as well as very large circles indeed, that represented the numerous fatalities of illegal immigrants caused by drowning, suffocation and freezing to death. Other publications are interested first and foremost in figures like inhabitants, household deficits and surpluses, or in the denominational composition of individual European countries; or else also in the position of the car industry in the states joining the EU, as well as in the most attractive metropolises of Europe. Those are obviously cities like London, Madrid, Amsterdam and Paris. It was already Paris for Benjamin and The Arcades Project. There, Benjamin talks not only about a city in general but rather about a city at a certain period – Paris during the 19th century. "Not all city life is modern; but all modern life is city life." writes Zygmunt Bauman. The places that I'm looking up are, with the exception of Istanbul, precisely the border districts, the peripheries - not so much of towns but more of countries. Thus in respect to the Zeitgeist, they are as a result to be seen as backward, although it is here that the politics of the European unification process finds its culmination.

However, the Schengen border is also already engraving itself into the 'inland'. Not only at airports, but also at stations and other sensitive domestic spots, there are more borders and more border police present than before. In Bergen, at the point from which the ferry to England sets sail and where it moors on its return, the harbour has recently been fenced in something like a fortress, and the quay where in the past I often used to go for a walk has been extensively enclosed. Now if you are a pedestrian, you have to take the busy road. That is also Europe – Norway is not a member of the EU but it is part of the Schengen agreement. England is a member of the EU but is not in the Schengen

Trinkgeld. Am Ende des Bosporus, am Schwarzem Meer, liegt auf der westlichen Seite eine europäische, das "Europäische Schloß" und auf der östlichen eine asiatische Festung, das "Anatolische Schloß". Am Grenzübergang in Ceuta, von Spanien nach Marokko, werde ich mit Steinen beschmissen. Eine meiner letzten Grenzsituationen wird wieder eine touristische sein: Die Riviera am Schwarzen Meer.

"Le Monde diplomatique" und der "Atlas der Globalisierung" stellten eine Karte Europas zusammen, die die Schengengrenze als klare rote Linie deutlich machte, und große und kleine, sowie sehr große Kreise darauf verteilte, die die zahlreichen Todesfälle durch Ertrinken, Ersticken, Erfrieren illegaler Einwanderer darstellten. Andere Zeitungen sind vor allem an Zahlen wie Einwohnern, Haushaltsdefiziten und -überschüssen oder an der konfessionellen Zusammensetzung der einzelnen europäischen Länder interessiert; oder auch an den Standorten der Automobilindustrie in den EU-Beitrittsländern, sowie den attraktivsten Metropolen Europas. Das sind natürlich Städte wie London, Madrid, Amsterdam und Paris. Paris war es bereits für Benjamin und sein Passagen-Werk. Benjamin spricht hier nicht über eine Stadt im allgemeinen, sondern über eine Stadt, in einer bestimmten Zeit: Paris, während des 19. Jahrhunderts. "Not all city life is modern; but all modern life is city life." schreibt Zygmunt Bauman. Die Orte, die ich aufsuche sind, mit der Ausnahme von Istanbuls, aber gerade die Randgebiete, die Peripherien nicht etwa von Städten, sondern von Ländern, sind also demnach in Hinsicht auf den Zeitgeist als rückständig zu betrachten, obwohl hier die Politik des europäischen Einigungsprozesses kulminiert.

Die Schengen-Grenze gräbt sich aber auch bereits ins "Inland". Nicht nur auf Flughäfen, auch an Bahnhöfen und anderen inländischen neuralgischen Punkten ist mehr Grenze und Grenzschutz präsent als zuvor. In Bergen ist neuerdings der Hafen festungsartig eingezäunt, dort wo die Fähre nach England an- und ablegt, ist der Kai, wo ich früher oft spazieren ging, großräumig umfriedet. Jetzt muss man als

agreement, therefore the Schengen border has to run around this state: fences, barbed wire, surveillance cameras, border police - who for security reasons stick to the continental mainland. Perhaps the last time that the harbour area in Bergen was so thoroughly controlled would have been during the Hanseatic days. Other ports too, as I became convinced of in Calais, where passengers, cars and lorries are shipped to the island of Britain, have been lavishly and thoroughly re-organised over recent years. All access and exit roads are fenced in, without shrubs or trees that might disturb a clear view and there are big manageable car parks and waiting areas and guards with Alsatians. Also, very close to Calais is situated the entrance for the TGV into the "Tunnel sous la Manche". From the bridge on the old main road between Boulogne-sur-Mer and Calais, I can watch the trains entering through several fences, bits of barbed wire and NATO wire. Surveillance cameras are positioned in a regular pattern. The railway tracks lie almost fifteen metres below, under the bridge. The four bored-out entrances are fenced off over an extensive area of the surrounding landscape. Floodlights are set at a close distance to one another. I am standing at the edge of a high security area. I also take a look at the TGV station in Frétun and then travel to the entrance for cars and lorries, a large toll checkpoint. I get out, and make some photos. Five boys overtake me and call to me: You take me to England!? Everything is lying in the chaos of a new way of managing the traffic, similar to a motorway, car parks and a trading estate in between, with an enormous gleaming silver metal clad tube, probably designed as a counterpart to the bore of the tunnel's pipe - the shopping centre "Cité Europe". Further on, on the main road past Sangatte, you already have a view over the Channel and you see the ferries crossing, and I once more pass by a fenced-in area, covered with high embankments and surveyed by video cameras, out of which jut green funnels. This is where the air passes in and out of the tunnel to ventilate it.

The European transformation process generates

Spaziergänger der stark befahrenen Straße folgen. Auch das ist Europa: Norwegen ist zwar nicht Mitglied der EU, aber des Schengen-Abkommens. England ist Mitglied der EU, aber nicht im Schengen-Abkommen, also muß um diesen Staat herum die Schengen-Grenze gezogen werden: Zäune, Stacheldraht, Überwachungskameras, Grenzschutz, der aus Sicherheitsgründen in kontinentales Festland sticht. Zum letzten Mal wird die Hafengegend in Bergen vielleicht zur Zeit der Hanse so gründlich kontrolliert worden sein. Auch andere Häfen, wie ich mich in Calais überzeugen konnte, wo Passagiere, Autos und Lastwagen auf die britische Insel verschifft werden, sind in den letzten Jahren aufwändig aufs Neue durchorganisiert worden. Alle Zu- und Abfahrten sind eingezäunt, keine Sträucher oder Bäume, die eine Übersichtlichkeit stören könnten, große überschaubare Park- und Warteplätze, Wachpersonal mit Schäferhunden. Ganz in der Nähe von Calais befindet sich auch die Einfahrt des TGV in den "Tunnel sous la Manche". Von der Überführung der alten Landstraße zwischen Boulogne-sur-Mer und Calais kann ich die Einfahrt der Züge durch mehrere Zäune, Stacheldraht und Nato-Draht hindurch beobachten. In regelmäßigem Raster sind Überwachungskameras plaziert. Die Eisenbahntrassen liegen fast fünfzehn Meter tiefer, unter der Brücke. Die vier Röhreneinfahrten sind großräumig in der umgebenden Landschaft abgezäunt. Flutlichtlampen stehen in engem Abstand. Ich stehe am Rande eines Hochsicherheitsgebietes. Ich schaue mir auch den TGV Bahnhof in Frétun an und fahre dann zur Einfahrt für Autos und LKWs, einer großen Mautstelle. Ich steige aus und mache Photos. Fünf Jungen überholen mich und rufen mir zu: You take me to England!? Alles liegt im Chaos einer neuen autobahnähnlichen Verkehrsführung, dazwischen Parkplätze und ein Gewerbegebiet mit einer riesigen silbernglänzenden metallverkleideten Röhre, wahrscheinlich als Pendant zur Tunnelröhre entworfen, das Einkaufszentrum "Cité Europe". Weiter, auf der Landstraße nach Sangatte von einer Anhöhe hat man schon einen Überblick

different, manifold, conflicting and incompatible images in its capital cities and at its borders. I am researching the sites of the peripheries. There, another present is alive. If, in previous projects, I have often imagined and dramatised the sites of the past through historical facts as well as fictions, then this time the sites I am selecting are synchronous to contemporary history. Perhaps the photos that I take at such a place are images that possess an historical index. And the images can be read as dialectics in a state of motionlessness.
Over the course of my various researches, Poland earns a special place, perhaps on behalf of other (south) east European countries. I know Poland above all in connection with the history of the Second World War, from history lessons that were no longer brought to life as vividly as the local history, geography and natural history lessons (Heimatkunde) had been before them. The high school's history books used maps, statistics and all variety of pictures in order to illustrate history, whereas Heimatkunde consisted mainly of excursions, unmediated experience, and history past and present. I want to go to the border in the east of Poland. Not in search of the traces of Nazi Germany, but rather because the Schengen boundary is being shifted as far as there. I would like to photograph this boundary. Before 1 May 2004! How do you travel through south east Poland? I don't have a clue. What towns lie that way? I have a chat with Marek. Krakow, Warsaw...no, further east, on the border...Przmysl...once you know how it's pronounced, then you have already understood the first rudiments of Polish pronunciation, and derived satisfaction from the sound of the language...Przmysl, yes that is just about the Ukraine, but also pretty far down in the south, what is there to the east? I go to bookshops and look for maps or travel guides. This region is scarcely mentioned. I look in the Internet. I get the most hits for websites dealing in the most diverse ways with Jewish history in this region. I know next to nothing about 'East European Jewry', 'ghettoes', 'shtetls' and so on. But south east Poland and then further down in the Ukraine, Lvov for example, which you reach

über den Kanal und man sieht die Fähren kreuzen, komme ich wieder an einem eingezäunten, von hohen Böschungen verdeckten und videoüberwachten Gelände, aus dem grüne Trichter ragen, vorbei. Hier wird der Tunnel be- und entlüftet.
Der europäische Transformationsprozess generiert unterschiedliche, mannigfaltige, gegensätzliche, unvereinbare Bilder in seinen Hauptstädten und an seinen Grenzen. Ich recherchiere die Orte der Ränder. Dort ist eine andere Gegenwart lebendig. Habe ich in früheren Projekten oft Orte der Vergangenheit durch historische Fakten wie auch Fiktionen vergegenwärtigt und dramatisiert, sind die Orte, die ich diesmal wähle, sychron zur gegenwärtigen Geschichte. Vielleicht sind die Photos, welche ich an so einem Ort mache, Bilder, die einen historischen Index haben. Und die Bilder kann man lesen, als Dialektik im Stillstand. Während meiner verschiedenen Recherchen, nimmt Polen einen besonderen Platz ein, vielleicht stellvertretend für andere (süd-) osteuropäische Länder. Polen kenne ich vor allem im Zusammenhang mit der Geschichte des Zweiten Weltkrieges, aus dem Geschichtsunterricht, der nicht mehr so anschaulich war wie davor die Heimatkunde. Die Geschichtsbücher des Gymnasiums benutzten Karten, Statistiken und Bilder aller Art, um Geschichte zu illustrieren. Wobei Heimatkunde hauptsächlich aus Exkursionen, unmittelbarer Erfahrung, vergangener und gegenwärtiger Geschichte bestand. Ich will an die Grenze im Osten Polens. Nicht auf der Suche nach den Spuren Nazideutschlands, sondern weil sich die Schengen-Grenze dorthin verschieben wird. Diese Grenze möchte ich photographieren. Vor dem 1. Mai 2004! Wie reist man durch Süd-Ost-Polen? Ich habe keine Ahnung. Welche Städte liegen dort? Ich unterhalte mich mit Marek. Krakau, Warschau ... nein weiter östlich, an der Grenze ... Przmysl ... wenn man einmal weiß wie es ausgesprochen wird, hat man schon die ersten Grundbegriffe polnischer Aussprache verstanden, und Gefallen am Klang der Sprache gefunden ... Przmysl, ja das ist fast Ukraine, aber auch schon sehr weit unten im Süden, was

directly from Przmysl, is the area that was earlier called Galicia and which today is traversed by three or four different countries. I enter the names of the smaller towns that I find on the map into the search engine. The first that pop up are the ones that have Jewish history. Sometimes they tell of life before the Second World War, but most often it is the story of the Second World War: Ghettoes, deportations, murders, forced labour, evacuation and extermination of the ghettoes, concentration camps, extermination of the Jewish population. To the east of Auschwitz, it was here that lay the big concentration camps of Majdanek, Sobibor and Belzec, at that time at a distance of only 150 to 200 km from each other. Eyewitness reports, lists of names of deported Jews, lists of names of murdered and missing Jews, lists of sponsors who contribute to the erection and upkeep of memorials. I find old photos, old city plans and maps. Sometimes a city website in Polish. I give up, I don't find anything current. I go to a bookshop and buy a good map of Poland. Germanwings has recently started flying to Warsaw. That's easy, direct from Cologne. Over the Internet once more, I hire a car to be picked up at Warsaw airport, look for a hotel and meet Katharina – she's coming from Leipzig with the train – at the 'Centralina' station on Easter Monday in Warsaw. She is to accompany me. In the coming days, we travel as close as we possibly can along the border in the east of Poland, from North to South. It doesn't take long before we have acclimatised ourselves. The lonely country roads, the farming with horses, the little villages, the storks' nests. This is all in the present, it is so rural that there is little that points to history. The wooden houses in the countryside, one storey high, sometimes a bit crooked, the ones nearby or in the villages somewhat more mixed, socialistic too, or also already renovated since the coming of the political change, particularly with new roofs. It is probably a region something like the fringe area of the FRG along the border with the GDR was previously. Rural, and in an unfavourable location, left to its own devices somewhat, poor, bit of a no-man's-land. Terespol, Wlodawa,

liegt im Osten? Ich gehe in Buchläden, suche nach Karten oder Reiseführern. Diese Gegend wird fast nicht erwähnt. Ich suche im Internet. Die meisten Treffer habe ich mit Websites, die die jüdische Geschichte in diesen Gebieten auf verschiedenste Weise bearbeiten. Ich weiß fast nichts über das "Ostjudentum", "Ghettos", "Schtetls" usw. Aber Süd-Ost-Polen und weiter unten in der Ukraine, Lvov zum Beispiel, wo man von Przmysl direkt hinkommt, ist die Gegend, die man früher Galizien nannte, die heute von drei oder vier verschiedenen Ländern durchteilt wird. Ich gebe in die Suchmaschinen die Namen der kleineren Städte ein, die ich auf der Landkarte finde. Es tauchen erstmal die auf, die jüdische Geschichte haben. Manchmal erzählen sie vom Leben vor dem Zweiten Weltkrieg, aber das meiste ist die Geschichte des Zweiten Weltkrieges: Ghettos, Deportationen, Ermordungen, Zwangsarbeit, Räumung und Vernichtung der Ghettos, Konzentrationslager, Vernichtung der jüdischen Bevölkerung. Östlich von Auschwitz, lagen hier die großen Konzentrationslager Majdanek, Sobibor und Belzec nur jeweils 150 bis 200 km voneinander entfernt. Augenzeugenberichte, Namenslisten von deportierten Juden; Namenslisten von ermordeten und vermißten Juden, Listen von Sponsoren, die spenden, um Gedenkstätten zu errichten und zu unterhalten. Ich finde alte Photos, alte Stadtpläne und Karten. Manchmal eine städtische Website auf polnisch. Ich gebe auf, ich finde nichts Gegenwärtiges. Ich gehe in einen Buchladen und kaufe eine gute Polenkarte. Germanwings fliegt neuerdings nach Warschau. Das ist einfach, direkt von Köln. Wieder übers Internet leihe ich ein Auto, das am Warschauer Flugplatz abzuholen ist, suche ich ein Hotel und treffe mich mit Katharina – sie kommt aus Leipzig mit dem Zug – am Bahnhof "Centralina" Ostermontag in Warschau. Sie begleitet mich. Die nächsten Tage fahren wir so nah wie möglich an der Grenze im Osten Polens entlang, von Norden nach Süden. Es dauert nicht lange und wir haben uns akklimatisiert. Die einsamen Landstrassen, der Ackerbau mit Pferden, die kleinen Dörfer, die Storchennester. Das ist alles Gegenwart, es ist so ländlich, dass wenig auf

Dorohushk, Budomierz, Skolin, Hrebenne, Medyka, Kroscienko were the names of the frontier stations here. In between lay Sobibor. If there was a sign standing by the side of the small country road, then we overlooked it. The landscape, the birches in sandy earth, the sun shining, the small roads on which for lengthy periods we did not encounter another car – all this lulled us to sleep somewhat and the name of the next place on our list is the name of a place at the border. There is a natural border here, the Bug, and controlled border crossings without much traffic from Terespol to Medyka. I'm looking for old ferry moorings or old (destroyed) bridges, but I don't find them here. On the contrary, the border stations are new or else were just recently expanded and strengthened.

In Dorohushk we leave the country road and drive down to the Bug. Past a new building that lies, fenced in, on a small hillock by the river. I stop and wind the window right down. On the cast-iron sign I read against the light something like 'Graniza'. I take a photograph from out of the car and we consider how we are going to drive on. At that point a soldier comes out of the gate, puts his cap on and of course approaches us. Get out of the car, papers, those of the car as well, the hire contract etc, open the boot and we are obliged to accompany him. Now we get to see the new building from inside. It is just being cleaned, it is early in the morning. Our passports and car papers are checked by telephone. While we are waiting, the boss of the station, a nice young man not in uniform, takes care of us. He asks us in a friendly manner what we are doing here. We explain a little, that we started from Warsaw, we are driving around a bit and are tourists and that we really like it here in this area. He apologises for his bad English and becomes somewhat embarrassed because he is holding tourists. Of course, everything is then in order with the papers and we are accompanied off the premises.

In Okopy at the border with Ukraine, a few private vehicles and lorries and two full car carriers are waiting. The tea-or-coffee kiosks, which mostly have a few tables and chairs standing outside, and the little offices, are almost empty.

Geschichte deutet, die Häuser auf dem Land aus Holz, eingeschossig, manchmal etwas schief, in der Nähe oder in den Dörfern etwas gemischter, sozialistisch auch, oder auch schon wieder nach der Wende renoviert, neue Dächer vor allem. Es ist wahrscheinlich so eine Region wie das frühere deutsche Zonenrandgebiet. Ländlich und ungünstig gelegen, ein wenig sich selbst überlassen, ärmlich, ein bisschen Niemandsland. Terespol, Wlodawa, Dorohushk, Budomierz, Skolin, Hrebenne, Medyka, Kroscienko heißen hier die Grenzstationen. Dazwischen lag Sobibor. Falls an der kleinen Landstrasse ein Schild gestanden hat, haben wir es übersehen. Die Landschaft, die Birken in sandigem Boden, die Sonne scheint, die kleinen Strassen, auf denen uns lange kein anderes Auto begegnet – das hat uns eingelullt und der Name des nächsten Ortes auf unserer Liste ist der eines Grenzortes. Es gibt hier die natürliche Grenze, den Bug, und kontrollierte Grenzübergänge, die von Terespol bis Medyka wenig Verkehr haben. Ich suche nach alten Fähranlegern oder alten (zerstörten) Brücken, die ich aber hier nicht finde. Im Gegenteil, die Grenzstationen sind neu oder werden gerade erweitert und ausgebaut.

In Dorohushk verlassen wir die Landstraße und fahren runter an den Bug. Vorbei an einem neuen Gebäude, das eingezäunt, auf einer kleinen Anhöhe, am Fluss liegt. Ich halte und drehe die Fensterscheibe ganz herunter. Auf dem gusseiserenen Schild lese ich im Gegenlicht etwas von "Graniza". Ich mache ein Photo, aus dem Auto heraus, und wir überlegen wie wir weiterfahren. Da kommt ein Soldat aus dem Tor, setzt seine Kappe auf und kommt natürlich auf uns zu. Aussteigen, Papiere, auch die vom Auto, den Leihvertrag etc, Kofferraum aufmachen und wir müssten mitkommen. Wir sehen nun das neue Gebäude von innen. Es wird gerade geputzt, es ist früh morgens. Unsere Pässe und die Autopapiere werden per Telefon gecheckt. Während der Wartezeit kümmert sich der Chef der Station, ein netter junger Mann, ohne Uniform um uns; er fragt uns freundlich, was wir hier machen. Wir erzählen ein bisschen, dass wir von Warschau aus etwas herumfahren und Touristen sind und es uns beiden hier in dem

A few people are standing about on the street. From far away you can see the actual border station, and all the way up to the border station is a building site. Suddenly we hear explosions and see smoke climbing out of the border patrol buildings, about 500m away as the crow flies. Then helicopters appear two or three times in the air and lower someone down. Otherwise everything remains peaceful – if all this was possibly just to do with a training exercise, we never discover.

Further south in Skolin, we're on the road early in the morning again, the village is situated directly on the border. We look for a path in a field leading to the border, but these always end earlier, at a field. The border must be somewhere beyond there, probably, marked like it was in Budomierz already, simply with a red and white Polish border post and a blue and yellow Ukrainian one. There are people in the fields, tilling their land with horse and tractor. On the way back to the village, my attention is drawn to an old deserted building directly on the road. I slow down a bit and over the entrance door see the perfectly round window. It has a window frame dividing it, made out of iron, rusted, that depicts a Star of David. I park the car and take a photo. On this side the building has two high storeys. I go back a bit and see the other face of the house. Here you can see from the high windows, likewise with round arches, that the space stretches over two floors. You can well comprehend the interior space from the exterior. It follows the inner division of a synagogue, the main room at the front and at the back two floors, of which the upper is the gallery for women. The roof is a flat hipped roof with rusted lead covering. I stand at the edge of the road and wait until the tractor and trailer has gone by in order to take photos, then a man speaks to me over the little garden fence at which I am standing: "You are zydowski ?" Just up to there, I don't know what that means and think he means photo journalist. I say that I am from Germany. He makes a disparaging movement of his hand and says something about Hitler...Wlodawa, Zamosc, Lubaszow, Lublin or Skolin are only a few villages or smaller towns

Landstrich gut gefällt. Er entschuldigt sich für sein schlechtes Englisch und wird etwas verlegen, weil er Touristen anhält. Mit den Papieren ist dann natürlich alles in Ordnung und wir werden aus dem Gelände hinausbegleitet.

In Okopy an der Grenze zur Ukraine, warten ein paar Pkw und Lkw und zwei volle Autotransporter. Die Tee- oder Kaffeekioske, die meistens ein paar Tische und Stühle draußen stehen haben, und die kleinen Büros sind fast leer. Ein paar Leute stehen auf der Straße herum. Von weitem sieht man die eigentliche Grenzstation, bis dorthin ist eine Baustelle; plötzlich hören wir Explosionen und sehen Rauch aufsteigen aus dem Grenzgebäude ca. 500 m Luftlinie entfernt. Dann kommen zwei-dreimal Hubschrauber durch die Luft und seilen jemanden ab. Ansonsten bleibt alles ruhig – ob es sich hier vielleicht nur um eine Übung handelte, finden wir nicht heraus.

Weiter südlich in Skolin sind wir wieder früh morgens unterwegs; das Dorf liegt direkt an der Grenze. Wir suchen einen Feldweg, der an die Grenze führt; die meisten enden aber immer schon vorher auf einem Feld. Dahinter müsste die Grenze sein, wahrscheinlich, wie schon in Budomierz einfach mit einem rot-weißen polnischen und einem blau-gelben ukrainischen Grenzpfahl markiert. Auf dem Acker sind Leute, die mit Pferd und Traktor ihr Feld bestellen. Auf dem Weg zurück ins Dorf fällt mir ein altes verlassenes Gebäude direkt an der Straße, auf. Ich fahre etwas langsamer und sehe über der Eingangstür das kreisrunde Fenster, es hat eine Fensterunterteilung aus Eisen, verrostet, die einen Davidsstern darstellt. Ich parke das Auto und mache ein Photo, auf dieser Seite hat das Gebäude zwei hohe Stockwerke, ich gehe ein Stück zurück und sehe die andere Front. Hier sieht man an den hohen Fenstern, ebenfalls mit Rundbögen, dass der Raum über zwei Etagen geht. Man kann gut die Innenräume dem Äußeren nachvollziehen. Es folgt der inneren Einteilung einer Synagoge, der Hauptraum vorne und hinten zwei Etagen, wobei die oberste die Frauenempore ist. Das Dach ist ein flaches Walmdach mit verrosteter Blecheindeckung. Ich

that we see. And where we become aware of the synagogues, more by chance than anything – although looked at in retrospect, they do have architectonic similarities: Historic, facades with pilaster and round arched windows and two-storeys. In Wlodawa there is a splendid building, fairly freshly renovated, which is today a museum and which has a large two-winged door with two seven armed candelabras stylised out of iron. In Lubaczow the locals draw our attention to the fact that the Polish postal building on the square was formerly the synagogue. In Zamosc, it is entered on the town plan next to the mikhwe, as it also is in Lublin. Today it accommodates a Jewish centre. Here in Skolin it lies abandoned without any road sign, like it probably was more than 60 years ago, situated on the through road and the little village square. I photograph the building because I have also already done that in the other places where the Europe of the Holocaust manifests itself. Or, for that matter, what about the Inquisition? Because on the surfer beach outside Tarifa, I am not sure if the hint of the skeletal reconstruction of a synagogue – in the ground is a big Star of David in intarsia in the plaster – on a piece of elevated land overlooking the Atlantic is an indication of the destruction wreaked by the Inquisition or that wreaked by the Holocaust. In Burgas, the local art museum has been accommodated within the former synagogue. I do not photograph this building. And without ever having raised any claim to being comprehensive, because that would in any case be a state of affairs endlessly impossible to oversee, this photo is one that I miss.

October 2004, at the end of the late summer season, I fly to Bulgaria in a Tupolev. I would like to photograph the borders to the north and to the south, as well as the Black Sea, the natural border in the East. Bulgaria, a candidate for entry into the EU since 1st May and consequently a potential Schengen state, is one of my last stops in the documentation of the border landscapes of Europe. The Villa List, a hotel that I have picked out of the brochure, lies thirty kilometres south of Burgas in Sozopol. My hotel lies outside of the old village in the newly

stehe am Strassenrand und warte bis der Trecker mit dem Anhänger vorbeigefahren ist, um Photos zu machen, da spricht mich ein Mann über den kleinen Gartenzaun, an dem ich stehe, an: “You are zydowski?” Ich weiß bis dahin noch nicht was das heißt, und denke er meint vielleicht Photoreporter, ich sage, ich sei aus Deutschland. Er macht eine leicht abfällige Handbewegung und sagt etwas über Hitler ... Wlodawa, Zamosc, Lubaszow, Lublin oder Skolin sind nur wenige Dörfer oder kleinere Städte, die wir sehen und mehr per Zufall auf die Synagogen aufmerksam werden – obwohl sie – im nachhinein betrachtet – architektonische Gemeinsamkeiten haben: historistisch, Fassaden mit Pilastern und Rundbogenfenstern, zweigeschossig. In Wlodawa ist es ein prächtiger Bau, ziemlich frisch renoviert, heute ein Museum und davor ein großes zweiflügeliges Tor, das aus Eisenstäben zwei siebenarmige Leuchter stilisiert, in Lubaczow machen uns die Einheimischen darauf aufmerksam, dass das Gebäude der polnischen Post am Platz früher die Synagoge war, in Zamosc ist sie neben der Mikhwe im Stadtplan eingetragen, so auch in Lublin und sie beherbergt heute ein jüdisches Zentrum; hier in Skolin liegt sie ohne Hinweisschild verlassen, wie wahrscheinlich vor mehr als 60 Jahren, an der Durchgangstraße und dem kleinen Platz des Dorfes. Ich photographiere das Gebäude, wie ich das auch schon in den anderen Orten an denen sich das Europa des Holocaust manifestiert, getan habe. Oder auch der Inquisition? Denn am Surferstrand vor Tarifa bin ich mir nicht sicher, ob der Hinweis der skeletthaften Rekonstruktion einer Synagoge – auf dem Boden ist ein großer Davidsstern in das Pflaster intarsiert – auf einer Anhöhe über dem Atlantik auf die Zerstörungen durch die Inquisition oder diejenigen des Holocaust hinweist. In Burgas ist in der ehemaligen Synagoge das lokale Kunstmuseum untergebracht worden. Dieses Gebäude photographiere ich nicht. Und ohne überhaupt einen Anspruch auf Vollständigkeit jemals erhoben zu haben, denn das wäre sowieso eine unendliche Unüberschaubarkeit, fehlt mir dieses Photo.

Oktober 2004- am Ende der Nachsaison fliege

constructed building area, on the bay, with a sea view. I have selected this as the site of departure for my excursions. It came to my attention during my postcard research in an antiquarian shop in Leipzig, where I bought postcards from the 60s and 70s since they vividly portrayed the construction and touristic situation on the Black Sea coast of Bulgaria, as well as of Romania. Judging from the postcards, only Nessebar and Sozopol are old, or very old, settlements. Sozopol possesses, in contrast to Nessebar, not as many old Thracian and Greek ruins, for here the postcards advertise their attractions by means of the typical Black Sea house, in which upper storeys sticking out like a collar and made of wood have been erected on a natural stone base one storey high. For several years, Sozopol has been conserved and restored through the means of the European programme for preservation of historic monuments. In Sozopol, a kind of 'Black Sea Fleet' is berthed in the military harbour. This tongue of land has already been used as a fortress and military base for thousands of years and today mainly mine ships are to be seen here. The Black Sea coast is divided into accessible and inaccessible terrains. Entrance to them was controlled, and still is today, because here either public beaches and camp sites, or private hotel beaches, as well as factories, ports, and military areas are differentiated from one another. The fishing boats set out early in the morning. On the horizon, a larger ship may sometimes be seen sailing slowly by.

On the morning after my nocturnal arrival, I pick up the hired car and set off immediately in a southerly direction towards Rezovo. Rezovo is marked on the map as a small place, in which the road ends shortly before the border with Turkey. For the first few days, I have good weather with sun, blue skies and midday heat, but then autumn arrives and later a raw burst of winter sets in. The country road runs past the villages of the Black Sea. In Tsarevo I drive off the country road and into the village, in order to see the coast and spy out the lie of the land. I photograph the sea and imagine the cartographic shape and the bordering countries to the north, south and east. I also walk through the

ich mit einer Tupolev nach Bulgarien. Ich möchte die Grenzen im Norden und Süden, sowie das Schwarze Meer, die natürliche Grenze im Osten, photographieren. Bulgarien, seit dem ersten Mai Beitrittskandidat der EU und folglich ein mögliches Schengen-Land, ist eine meiner letzten Stationen, die Grenzlandschaften Europas zu dokumentieren. Die Villa List, ein Hotel, das ich aus dem Katalog herausgesucht habe, liegt dreißig Kilometer südlich von Burgas in Sozopol. Mein Hotel liegt außerhalb des alten Dorfes im Neubaugebiet, an der Bucht, mit Meerblick. Den Ort habe ich mir als Ausgangspunkt für meine Exkursionen gewählt. Auf ihn aufmerksam wurde ich bei meiner Postkartenrecherche in einem Antiquariat in Leipzig, wo ich Postkarten der 60er und 70er Jahre gekauft habe, da sie die bauliche und touristische Situation an der Schwarzmeerküste Bulgariens sowie Rumäniens anschaulich wiedergeben. Nach den Postkarten zu urteilen, sind nur Nessebar und Sozopol alte, sehr alte Ansiedlungen. Sozopol hat im Gegensatz zu Nessebar nicht so viele alte Ruinen der Thraker und Griechen, denn hier werben die Postkarten mit dem typischen Schwarzmeerhaus, bei dem auf einen geschoßhohen Natursteinsockel auskragende Holzobergeschosse aufgebaut sind. Sozopol wird seit einigen Jahren mit Mitteln der europäischen Denkmalpflege erhalten und restauriert. In Sozopol liegt eine Art "Schwarzmeerfloote" im Militärhafen. Die Landzunge wird schon seit Jahrtausenden als Festung und militärischer Stützpunkt genutzt und heute sieht man hier hauptsächlich Minenboote. Die Schwarzmeerküste ist unterteilt in zugängliche und unzugängliche Gebiete. Der Zutritt wurde und wird auch heute noch kontrolliert, weil hier entweder öffentliche Strände und Campingplätze, oder private Hotelstrände als auch Fabriken, Häfen und Militärgebiete gegeneinander abgegrenzt sind. Früh morgens fahren die Fischerboote raus, am Horizont sieht man manchmal ein größeres Schiff langsam vorbeifahren.

Am Morgen nach meiner nächtlichen Ankunft hole ich den Leihwagen ab und mache mich sofort auf, in südliche Richtung, nach Rezovo.

village and in the centre stands a monument consisting of three ten metre high stone figures – soldier, worker and peasant woman – man in coat with rifle, man with ship's propeller, woman with fruit. I photograph it from three sides. In front of the houses are lying heaps of wood that still has to be cut and split in order to heat the winter stove. Some people are busy chopping it up with an axe or have put a circular saw in front of their house. You can also see wood suppliers, who offer this inclusive service and deal with everything immediately, on the spot. Ten kilometres further on, I make an additional digression to the bank of Ahtopol and here photograph the sea and the horizon. To the left, on the last rocky cliff in the sea, stands a lighthouse. I drive on.

Between Sinemorets and Rezovo is what's called "Border Area", however there are still 25 kilometres to drive until the end of the road. It leads away from the sea and somewhat into the mountains. The road has a lot of potholes and in the final kilometres almost turns into a forest path. There I see a control post, at some distance away – a barrier and a wooden shack, next to it a car belonging to the border police. I naturally think that my journey is to end here – in the middle of the forest – it could be forbidden to travel on as far as the border. The patrol stops me, I have to show my passport and to my surprise, the barrier is raised manually. I drive on and a short while later, I see the first houses, an old abandoned school, gardens. It goes downhill a bit, and up ahead the Black Sea appears in view. At the end of the road, I park the car, an old watchtower stands on the rocks ahead of me. I get out and take my camera with me. There is no-one to be seen. Concealed, I take a few photos of the watchtower. It is very still. I have the sense that I am being watched, of being at a strictly monitored border. There is a bar on the corner. I go in there first of all. It is dark inside. I order a tea and take the cup up into the fresh air on the terrace on the second floor. It's like being on a watchtower here, you have a good view over the landscape. To the left, at the front, the watchtower, standing on the fenced-in piece of land right by the rocky cliffs, opposite a small

Rezovo ist auf der Landkarte als kleiner Ort, in dem die Straße kurz vor der Grenze zur Türkei endet, eingezeichnet. Die ersten Tage habe ich schönes Wetter mit Sonne, blauem Himmel und heißen Mittagen, aber dann wird der Herbst und später ein rauher Winter einbrechen. Die Landstraßne führt an den Dörfern des Schwarzen Meeres vorbei. In Tsarevo fahre ich von der Landstraße ab in das Dorf, um die Küste zu sehen und auszukundschaften. Ich photographiere das Meer und stelle mir die kartographische Form und die Anrainerstaaten im Norden, Süden und Osten vor. Ich gehe auch durch das Dorf und im Zentrum steht ein Monument aus drei zehn Meter hohen Steinfiguren – Soldat, Arbeiter und Bäuerin – Mann in langem Mantel mit Gewehr, Mann mit Schiffsschraube, Frau mit Obst. Ich photographiere es von drei Seiten. Vor den Häusern liegen Haufen von Holz, das noch geschnitten und gespalten werden muss, um die Öfen im Winter zu heizen. Manche Leute sind dabei, es mit der Axt zu zerhacken oder haben sich eine Kreissäge vor das Haus gestellt, man sieht auch Holzlieferanten, die diesen Service inklusive anbieten und alles sofort an Ort und Stelle erledigen. Zehn Kilometer weiter mache ich zusätzlich einen Abstecher ans Ufer von Ahtopol und photographiere auch hier das Meer und den Horizont. Links auf der letzten Felsenklippe im Meer steht ein Leuchtturm. Ich fahre weiter.

Zwischen Sinemorets und Rezovo ist "Border Area", es sind aber noch 25 Kilometer bis zum Ende der Straße zu fahren. Es geht vom Meer weg etwas ins Gebirge. Die Straße hat viele Schlaglöcher und wird auf den letzten zehn Kilometern fast zum Waldweg. Da sehe ich in einiger Entfernung einen Kontrollposten – einen Schlagbaum und eine Bretterbude, daneben das Auto der Grenzpolizei. Ich denke natürlich, daß meine Fahrt hier enden wird – mitten im Wald – bis an die Grenze zu fahren, könnte verboten sein. Die Patrouille hält mich an, ich muß meinen Paß zeigen und zu meiner Überraschung wird der Schlagbaum per Handbetrieb hochgestellt. Ich fahre weiter und kurze Zeit später sehe ich die ersten Häuser, eine alte verlassene kleine Schule, Gärten. Es geht ein bißchen berg-

orthodox church, next to that a garden with a Bulgarian flag blowing in the wind. Then further to the right, the land declines down to a bay - here is the mouth of the river, which is simultaneously the border river between Turkey and Bulgaria, and on the other side, the other bank, there too a watch tower, and in the background minarets can be distinguished. I take a couple more surreptitious photos. From up here I have a good overview, but no good camera position. Then I hear voices and three people walk between the church and garden and onto the edge of the cliff. They lean against the railings and take photographs of each other in front the Black Sea. I understand immediately and am relieved – photographing is actually not a problem. I promptly leave the terrace, take a look inside the church, continue on to the railings, in order from here - it's an old surveillance path and trench - to assess the situation anew and begin to photograph. The trench snakes its way along the cliffs to the watchtower. Fixed onto a fence, in capital letters in the colour of the Bulgarian flag – white, green, red – is the name Bulgaria in Cyrillic script. On the other side, the land goes abruptly downhill and below you can see the mouth of the little river, a few boats and cars. On this side of the river there stands a big sign indicating Bulgarian territory, on the other side a sign with a white half moon and star on a red background; this is where something begins that was already to be seen from the viewing terrace of the bar – the Turkish shore. The surface of the sea in the bay between Bulgaria and Turkey gleams and glitters in the sun. I go back and forward along the surveillance path and now photograph the lot. When I stand still one time, the man from the small group addresses me and explains to me that he is from Stuttgart, of Bulgarian origin and that he is looking for a nice bit of land on the Black Sea. He asks if I'm not looking for something, too. He goes on to tell me how heavily watched this spot had been in earlier times and that you couldn't come this far at all without a special permit. The atmosphere of observation still hung in the air, I'd noticed that myself. We take our leave of each other. The sun, against which I

ab, vorne taucht das Schwarze Meer auf. Am Ende der Straße parke ich das Auto, vorne am Felsen steht ein alter Wachturm. Ich steige aus und nehme die Kamera mit. Es sind keine Leute zu sehen. Versteckt mache ich ein paar Photos vom Wachturm. Es ist sehr still. Ich habe das Gefühl beobachtet zu werden, an einer streng überwachten Grenze zu sein. An der Ecke ist eine Kneipe, ich gehe erstmal da rein. Drinnen ist es dunkel, ich bestelle einen Tee und gehe mit der Tasse in die frische Luft auf die Terrasse in der zweiten Etage. Hier, es ist wie auf einem Wachturm, hat man einen guten Überblick: links vorne der Wachturm, der auf einem eingezäunten Grundstück direkt an der Felsenklippe steht, gegenüber eine kleine orthodoxe Kirche, daneben ein Garten mit einer im Wind wehenden bulgarischen Flagge, dann weiter rechts geht es hinunter an eine Bucht, hier ist die Mündung des Flusses, der gleichzeitig Grenzfluß zwischen der Türkei und Bulgarien ist und auf der anderen Seite das andere Ufer, auch dort sind ein Wachturm und im Hinterland Minarette zu erkennen. Ich mache wieder versteckt ein paar Photos. Von hier oben habe ich einen guten Überblick, aber keine gute Kameraposition. Dann höre ich Stimmen und drei Leute gehen zwischen Kirche und Garten an den Rand der Klippe. Sie stellen sich an das Geländer und photographieren sich dann gegenseitig vor dem Schwarzen Meer. Ich verstehe sofort und bin erleichtert; photographieren ist doch kein Problem. Ich verlasse unverzüglich die Terrasse, schaue in die Kirche hinein, gehe weiter an das Geländer, um von hier aus, es ist ein alter Wachweg und Schützengraben, die Situation von neuem zu überschauen und fange an zu photographieren. Der Schützengraben schlängelt sich an der Steilküste entlang zum Wachturm. An einem Zaun ist in großen Buchstaben in der Farbe der bulgarischen Flagge – weiß, grün, rot – der Name Bulgaria in kyrillischer Schrift angebracht. Auf der anderen Seite geht es schroff steil bergab und unten sieht man die Mündung des kleinen Flusses, ein paar Boote und Autos. Auf dieser Seite des Flusses steht ein großes Schild, das auf bulgarisches Territorium hinweist, auf der anderen Seite ein

would have had to photograph, has disappeared behind a cloud once more and I would like to carry on taking photos. When the sun comes out again, I sun myself a bit, leaning on the railings, and look around me on all sides one more time, in case I have overlooked something, then set off on the way back. I can only take the same route that I arrived on. I stop briefly on the sandy beach of Dyuni and take another few photos of the horizon of the Black Sea. I get back to Sozopol in twilight, my memory stick is full, and before I am able think about anything else, I load the pictures onto my hard drive in the hotel. Early tomorrow morning, I want to travel in the same direction again, higher up into the mountains to a border crossing between Bulgaria and Turkey, near Malko Tarnovo.
This time in Tsarevo, the route goes up into the mountains. The narrow country road leads for almost 60 kilometres through oak woods and I only rarely pass through a village. The road is once again full of potholes. Even though I have to a certain extent exercised some foresight as to the time of this journey, it is still tiring. Shortly before Gramatikova, about 25 kilometres from Malko Tarnovo or 35 kilometres before the Turkish border, the so-called 'Border Area' commences again and border police stop me, control and register my papers and allow me to continue on my way. Before Malko Tarnovo, the road forks - to the right it goes into the town and to the left into Turkey. Istanbul is 286 kilometres away. I take the road into the mountains and drive past deserted border outposts, waiting areas, control huts and control cars to the actual present day border patrol. – There, in front of me. – I park the car well away from the first barrier, take the camera off the back seat and take a few photos. The sun is shining in such a way that the subjects – transmitter mast, control huts, barrier – are set against the light. I can see that the road behind the barrier makes a bend. Perhaps there is a service area there, for drinking a coffee and taking more photos. Since for legal insurance reasons I cannot drive the hire car over the border, I leave it parked and continue on foot. The border official controls my passport and

Schild mit weißem Halbmond und Stern auf rotem Grund; hier beginnt, was man schon von der Aussichtsterrasse der Kneipe gesehen hat: Das türkische Ufer. Die Meeresoberfläche in der Bucht zwischen Bulgarien und der Türkei glänzt und funkelt in der Sonne. Ich gehe den Wachweg hin und her und photographiere das jetzt alles. Als ich einmal stehen bleibe, spricht mich der Mann der kleinen Gruppe kurz an und erzählt mir, dass er aus Stuttgart ist, bulgarischer Herkunft, und er sucht ein schönes Grundstück am Schwarzen Meer. Ob ich auch etwas suche, fragt er. Er erzählt mir noch, wie scharf bewacht diese Stelle früher gewesen sei und dass man gar nicht ohne Sondergenehmigung bis hierher kam. Die Stimmung der Überwachung, das habe ich selbst gemerkt, liegt immer noch in der Luft. Wir verabschieden uns. Die Sonne, die nun im Gegenlicht steht, ist wieder hinter einer Wolke verschwunden und ich möchte weitere Photos machen. Als die Sonne wieder rauskommt, sonne ich mich ein bißchen am Geländer lehnend, schaue mich nach allen Seiten noch einmal um, ob ich irgendetwas übersehen habe und mache mich dann auf den Rückweg. Ich kann nur die gleiche Strecke wie die Hinfahrt nehmen. Ich halte kurz am Sandstrand von Dyuni und mache noch ein paar Photos vom Horizont des Schwarzen Meeres. In der Dämmerung bin ich zurück in Sozopol, mein Memory Stick ist voll und bevor ich an irgendetwas anderes denken kann, lade ich im Hotel die Bilder auf meine Festplatte. Morgen früh will ich wieder in die gleiche Richtung, weiter hoch ins Gebirge an einen Grenzübergang zwischen Bulgarien und der Türkei in der Nähe von Malko Tarnovo.
Bei Tsarevo geht es diesmal ins Gebirge. Die schmale Landstraße führt fast 60 Kilometer durch Eichenwälder und nur selten komme ich durch ein Dorf. Die Straße hat wieder viele Schlaglöcher. Auch wenn ich mit der Zeit für sie eine gewisse Voraussicht entwickelt habe, ist die Fahrt anstrengend. Kurz vor Gramatikova, ca. 25 km vor Malko Tarnovo oder 35 Kilometer vor der türkischen Grenze, fängt wieder die sogenannte "Border Area" an und Grenzpolizei hält mich an, kontrolliert und registriert meine Papiere und lässt mich weiterfahren. Vor Malko

gestures towards the car. I explain to him the reason why I have left it standing, but I don't think he understands it; only that I want to go for a coffee. He bangs an exit stamp into my passport, gives it back and shuts his little window again. The coffee shop past the curve is shut. I walk slowly and turn around a few times in order to take photos. As inconspicuously as possible, but here, I now have the sun behind me. I change sides of the road in order to obtain another angle of vision, and from here take some further photos of the curve in the road, of the coffee shop sign, of the transmitter mast, of the tree that has just begun to bud, and of the forest in the background. I slowly approach, step by step, the control point 200 metres away on the next curve. It is the Bulgarian Customs, here luggage and cars belonging to those travelling across get a going-over. I go past there without being stopped. I am surprised that I am not observed at all. I carry on taking photos, as inconspicuously as possible – walk slowly, turn around briefly, look through the viewfinder and depress the shutter – once, twice, thrice and walk slowly on. My digital camera's technical procedure for taking a photograph is recognisable through the sounds it emits. The camera resounds with a pling plong pling when being set; when focusing, it goes duhduh dut and when shooting, it makes a fake mirror reflex trigger noise. Of course, you can programme these sounds to be switched off, but I find them helpful in these sometimes slightly tense situations. The sequence of sounds structures the virtual. The next thing I encounter is a big trapezium shaped lead box a bit like a garage. I also see a controller there. I go towards him, since I suspect that there is another passport control here. He waves me on however and I am so close that I can make out that "water" is standing in the "garage" and that only cars drive through here because of foot-and-mouth disease. I walk on, and turn around again in order to take photos – the Bulgarian Customs with flags now in the background, to the right the "garage", like this I still have the sun at my back. In front of me now is the Turkish flag and, on a sign over the road, 'welcome' written in Turkish, plus an English

Tarnovo gabelt sich die Straße, rechts geht es in den Ort und links in die Türkei. Istanbul ist 286 Kilometer entfernt. Ich nehme die Straße ins Gebirge und fahre an verlassenen Grenzvorposten, Warteplätzen, Kontrollhäuschen und Kontrollwagen vorbei zum eigentlichen heutigen Grenzstreifen. – Da vorne. – Den Wagen parke ich weit vor dem ersten Schlagbaum, nehme die Kamera vom Rücksitz und mache ein paar Photos. Die Sonne scheint so, dass die Motive – Sendemast, Kontrollhäuschen, Schlagbaum – im Gegenlicht stehen. Ich sehe, dass die Straße hinter dem Schlagbaum einen Knick macht. Vielleicht gibt es dort eine Raststätte, um Kaffee zu trinken und weitere Photos zu machen. Da ich den Leihwagen aus versicherungsrechtlichen Gründen nicht über die Grenze fahren darf, lasse ich ihn stehen und gehe zu Fuß weiter. Der Grenzbeamte kontrolliert meinen Reisepass und macht eine Andeutung zum Auto. Ich erkläre ihm den Grund, warum ich ihn stehenlasse, den er aber, glaube ich, nicht versteht; nur, dass ich Kaffee trinken gehen will. Er knallt einen Ausreisestempel in meinen Pass, gibt ihn zurück, und schließt sein Fensterchen wieder. Der Coffee-Shop hinter der Kurve hat geschlossen. Ich gehe langsam und drehe mich ein paarmal um, um Photos zu machen. Möglichst unauffällig, aber hier habe ich jetzt die Sonne im Rücken. Ich wechsele die Straßenseite, auch um einen anderen Blickwinkel zu erhalten und mache von hier aus weitere Photos von der Straßenkurve, dem Schild des Coffee-Shops, vom Sendemast, vom Baum, der gerade Knospen bekommen hat, und von dem Wald im Hintergrund. Ich nähere mich langsam, schrittweise dem 200 Meter entfernten Kontrollpunkt in der nächsten Kurve. Es ist der bulgarische Zoll, hier werden Gepäck und Autos der Durchreisenden auseinandergenommen. Ich gehe daran vorbei, ohne angehalten zu werden. Ich wundere mich, daß man mich gar nicht beachtet. Ich mache weiter, so unauffällig wie möglich, Photos – gehe langsam, drehe mich kurz um, schaue durch den Sucher und drücke auf den Auslöser – einmal, zweimal, dreimal, und gehe langsam weiter. Der technische Ablauf des Photographierens meiner digitalen Kamera ist durch Soundzeichen

'Welcome' and behind that, the Turkish passport control. Shortly afterwards comes the Customs and the Duty Free Zone with a store and a snack bar, which is entirely empty. I go in, but there is moreover no-one there who could serve me. I walk on, I am taking photos. Earlier, I saw on the map that this border crossing is situated at a height of almost 700 metres. On this side of the border, the land goes downhill again – the exit lies ahead. I turn around once more to take a photo, and at that moment a man addresses me from behind: Taxi!? I'm a bit startled, what taxi, where to!? He points it out – back there is the way out of this walled-in, in-between zone, and down the hill is the way to...he names a name, perhaps the next village, I now think, and say "No! No!" He repeats Taxi!?? We go back and forth for a while, I say "Thank you" and set off in the opposite direction. Behind the fence on the right two soldiers have been watching us. I would have liked to have asked the taxi driver how much it costs to Istanbul but wanted to avoid further discussion. I just click quickly through the photos that I have shot up until now, as a control, and set off on the way back to the car. Back past the Turkish Customs and Duty Free Shop – on the welcome sign from this side it reads in white lettering on a red background "Güle Güle" and "Good Bye". I take a quick photo and walk on. At the Bulgarian Customs on this side stand a few cars from Romania and Turkey. This time the officials speak to me and I am asked what that is supposed to be about, taking a walk over the border, why I just went over and now came back already and so on; they're surly, maybe they feel a bit like they are being made fun of and they check my passport. My camera, though, I hide somewhat behind my arm, since one of them is looking me up and down, searching for a larger bag or something similar. Even more bad-temperedly he returns my passport to me – he has no reason to stop me. The road makes this gentle curve and I am out of sight. I photograph the corner with the coffee shop once more and the transmitter mast and once again reach the Bulgarian Passport Control. Only reluctantly do they too give me an entry stamp in my passport.

wiedererkennbar: beim Anstellen der Kamera ertönt ein pling-plong-pling, beim Fokussieren düddeldüt, beim Abdrücken ein gefaktes Spiegel-Auslöser-Geräusch. Diese Geräusche kann man natürlich im Programm ausschalten, aber ich finde sie hilfreich bei diesen manchmal etwas angespannten Situationen. Die Klangabfolge strukturiert das Virtuelle. Ich komme als nächstes an eine große garagenähnliche Trapezblechbox und sehe auch dort einen Kontrolleur. Ich gehe auf ihn zu, da ich vermute, dass hier wieder eine Passkontrolle ist. Er winkt mich aber weiter und ich bin so nah, dass ich erkennen kann, dass "Wasser" in der "Garage" steht und hier nur Autos durchfahren wegen der Maul- und Klauenseuche. Ich gehe weiter und drehe mich wieder um, um Photos zu machen – hinten jetzt der bulgarische Zoll mit Fahnen, rechts die "Garage", die Sonne habe ich so immer noch im Rücken. Vor mir jetzt die türkische Flagge und auf einem Schild über der Straße ein Willkommen auf Türkisch und Welcome, dahinter die türkische Passkontrolle. Kurz darauf der Zoll und die Duty Free Zone mit einem Geschäft und einem Imbiss, der ganz leer ist. Ich gehe hinein, aber es ist auch niemand da, der bedienen könnte. Ich gehe weiter, ich mache Photos. Ich habe vorher auf der Karte gesehen, dass sich dieser Grenzübergang auf fast 700 Meter Höhe befindet. Es geht auf dieser Seite der Grenze wieder bergab – da vorne liegt der Ausgang, ich drehe mich wieder herum, um ein Photo zu machen, da spricht mich ein Mann von hinten an: Taxi!? Ich erschrecke mich, wie Taxi, wohin? Er zeigt 'raus – dahinten ist der Ausgang aus diesem eingemauerten Zwischenraum, den Berg runter, geht es nach ... er nennt einen Namen, vielleicht das nächste Dorf, denke ich jetzt, und sage No!No!, er wiederholt Taxi!?? Es geht ein bißchen hin- und her, ich sage Thank you und mache mich auf in die entgegengesetzte Richtung. Hinter dem Zaun rechts, haben uns zwei Soldaten beobachtet. Ich hätte den Taxifahrer gerne gefragt, was es bis Istanbul kostet, wollte aber weitere Diskussionen vermeiden. Ich klicke noch schnell zur Kontrolle die bis hierhin geschossenen Photos durch und mache mich auf den Rückweg zum Auto. Wieder

I go back to the car, am somewhat exhausted from the mental strain of the anxiety of being watched, being sent away, getting an order forbidding me to photograph, or even that someone could have taken the camera away from me. I put the camera down on the backseat of the car, start up the engine, turn around and drive back to Malko Tarnovo, where I don't take the direct route to the Black Sea but instead drive further west through the Strandzha mountains, and not until I am towards the east past Kroushevets do I come back to Sozopol on a side road with even more potholes. In Kroushevets a garden restaurant has opened. It is hot, already three o'clock and I am hungry and order cevapcici with potatoes and ayran. A long distance coach stops in the car park behind the garden and is quickly full up. The coach covers the stretch Bucharest - Istanbul.

During my investigations and travels I was grateful to come across the following books:

Jurij Andruchowytsch, Das letzte Territorium, Suhrkamp, Frankfurt 2003;
Andruchowytsch/Stasiuk, Mein Europa, Suhrkamp, Frankfurt 2004;
Zygmunt Bauman, Life in Fragments, Blackwell Publishers, Oxford 1995;
Ulrich Beck und Edgar Grande, Das kosmopolitische Europa, Suhrkamp, Frankfurt 2004;
Christine Buci-Glucksmann, Der kartographische Blick der Kunst, Merve Verlag, Berlin 1988;
David Crouch and Nina Lübbren (ed.), Visual Culture and Tourism, Berg, Oxford 2003;
Michel de Certeau, Die Kunst des Handelns, Merve Verlag, Berlin 1987;
Michel Mollat du Jourdin, Europa und das Meer, C.H. Beck, München 1993;
Sven Lindquist, Wüstentaucher, Unionsverlag, Berlin 2004;
Peter Sloterdijk, Falls Europa erwacht, Suhrkamp, Frankfurt 2002.

am türkischen Zoll und Duty Free Shop vorbei – auf dem Willkommensschild heißt es von dieser Seite in weißer Schrift auf rotem Grund Güle Güle und Good Bye. Ich mache ein schnelles Photo und gehe weiter. Am bulgarischen Zoll stehen auf dieser Seite ein paar Autos aus Rumänien und der Türkei. Diesmal werde ich von den Beamten angesprochen und gefragt, was das soll, durch die Grenze zu spazieren, warum ich eben darüber und jetzt schon wieder zurückkomme usw.; man ist mürrisch, sie fühlen sich vielleicht ein bisschen zum Narren gehalten und checken den Reisepass, meine Kamera verstecke ich ein bisschen hinter dem Arm, denn einer mustert mich, nach einer größeren Tasche oder etwas ähnlichem suchend. Noch mißmutiger gibt er mir den Pass zurück – er hat keinen Grund mich anzuhalten. Die Straße macht diese sanfte Kurve und ich bin außer Sichtweite, ich photographiere nochmal die Ecke mit dem Coffee Shop und dem Sendemast und erreiche wieder die bulgarischen Passkontrolleure. Nur widerwillig machen auch sie mir den Einreisestempel in meinen Reisepass. Ich gehe zurück zum Auto, bin etwas erschöpft, von der Anspannung beobachtet zu werden, weggeschickt zu werden, ein Photographier-Verbot zu bekommen, oder dass sogar jemand mir die Kamera abnehmen könnte. Ich lege die Kamera nach hinten auf den Rücksitz, lasse den Wagen an, drehe und fahre zurück bis Malko Tarnovo, wo ich nicht die direkte Straße ans Schwarze Meer nehme, sondern weiter westlich durch das Strandzha Gebirge fahre und erst hinter Kroushevets nach Osten über eine Nebenstraße mit noch mehr Schlaglöchern nach Sozopol zurückkomme. In Kroushevets hat ein Gartenlokal geöffnet. Es ist heiß, schon drei Uhr und ich habe Hunger und bestelle Cevapcici mit Kartoffeln und Ayran. Es hält ein Fernreisebus auf dem Parkplatz hinter dem Garten und es wird kurz voll. Der Bus befährt die Strecke Bukarest-Istanbul.

Doris Frohnapfel

Picture Postcards

Index – from left to right

[207]
1 Rovinj – Yugoslavia
2 Olimp – Romania
3 Vösu – Estonia
4 Nessebar – Bulgaria
5 Odessa – Ukraine
6 The artic circle – Norway
7 Varna, Golden Sands – Bulgaria
8 Mamaia – Romania
9 Primorsko – Bulgaria
10 Dinard, La Promenade des Alliés – France
11 Varna – Bulgaria
12 Palanga, The Pier – Lithuania
13 Psvikelv – Norway
14 Soci – CCCP, Black Sea
15 Camping Kranewo – Bulgaria
16 Jelsa – Yugoslavia
17 Nessebar – Bulgaria
18 Old boats at the Dune in Nida – Lithuania
19 Varna – Bulgaria
20 Spitsbergen – Norway
21 The Mosque of Dolmabahce and the Bosporus – Turkey

[208]
22 Slatni Pjassyzi – Bulgaria
23 Sopot – Poland
24 Grense Jakobselv – Norway
25 Slantschev, The Hotel Europe – Bulgaria
26 Salve Bridge, Bilbao – Basque Country
27 Ghajn Tuffieha Bay – Malta
28 Dubrovnik – Yugoslavia
29 The Fortress and Bosporus – Turkey
30 Renskiljning – Lappland
31 Kap Kaliakra – Bulgaria
32 Mamaia – Romania
33 Ørje, Grensen Kro & Vertshus – Norway
34 Narva – Estonia
35 Passenger terminal, Riga – Latvia
36 White cliffs of Dover – England
37 Lauluväljak, Tallinn – Estonia
38 Ferry at The Danube, Vac – Hungary
39 Nessebar – Bulgaria
40 Crikvenika – Yugoslavia
41 Sozopol – Bulgaria
42 The Europe Bridge, Istanbul – Turkey

[209]
43 Arminza, Vizcaya – Basque Country
44 The Danube, Kloster Weltenburg – Germany
45 Postira – Yugoslavia
46 Soci – CCCP, Black Sea
47 Constancia – Romania
48 Wladystanow – Poland
49 Bergen, Fishmarket – Norway
50 Nessebar – Bulgaria
51 The Rock from spanish shore – Gibraltar
52 The seaside near Riga – Latvia
53 Saint Cast, Pointe extreme – France
54 Luftbrückendenkmal, Berlin – Germany
55 Camping Coop, Burgas – Bulgaria
56 Nessebar, the harbour – Bulgaria
57 Trogir – Yugoslavia
58 Picos de Europa – Spain
59 Inari Lake – Finland
60 Dubrovnik – Yugoslavia
61 Sozopol – Bulgaria
62 Pirovac – Yugoslavia
63 The highest point on the Tyin, Årdal Road, Alt. 3665 feet – Norway

All images are from my postcard collection

KAR10

Email interviews

Passport • Email interview with Thierry Geoffroy (France-Denmark)

Dear Thierry, at the beginning of the 90s, we exhibited in the same space in (East-) Berlin: "Fotogalerie in der Brotfabrik" which was then curated by Inka Schube. This year, I invited you to the Academy in Bergen to show your work and teach the students. You came from Copenhagen, and you were late arriving from the airport in Bergen because the Norwegian police took you out to check you and you told me that that often happens to you. I have travelled back and forth between Germany and Scandinavia countless times the last 5 years and it actually never happened to me, with my German passport. What kind of passport do you have?

Thierry Geoffroy: A French passport.

DF: Norway is part of "Europe's Schengen zone of easy cross-border travel without identity check" ... "The benefits to air travellers have been swiftly apparent now that they can move within Schengenland without customs or passports checks." Here, and at any other internal Schengen-Border, how does it feel nowadays to be picked out and what reasons are there?

TG: For me to be picked up proves that I exist. The customs people saw me as a different person, therefore suspect. I rather take this as a compliment and it gave me as a foreigner an occasion to have a conversation of some kind with some Norwegian people. Except for the customs people, nobody will come to me and get curious about who I am in the streets of Bergen (apart from the police, maybe).
I got to meet 2 Norwegian customs guys looking in my pockets, asking me what was this and that, looking in my purse. It was like making a kind of retrospective work about what I carry with me when I am on a short journey. They found a small sock from my boy, some old biscuits, they really got suspicious when they discovered a small paper that concealed a memory card for my camera. Memories can be carried around, so can my Latin looks, you cannot avoid that.
Schengen border or non-borders is just another word that does not mean what it proclaims to contain, like many other words. Like most words used.
Personally I don't mind to be searched.
I like the idea of passage, of entering a different place, with an effect.
In art I use the concept of delivering visas if people want to visit some of my art. I don't want anybody to enter and consume anything of what I am doing, I ask them to fill in visa forms, or to fill in a questionnaire that they have to pass successfully, as a test.
Control can be an act of communication, curiosity and interest, it is almost better than being indifferent and tolerant, ignoring that others exist.
Yes, I think those border officers picked me up because they wanted to know which kind of traveller I was, and I can understand that curiosity. I told them I was on a teaching trip. They got even more curious and maybe suspicious. A guy like me on a teaching trip could be of a greater danger for the Norwegian people, even!
In most towns, the doors have a protection system, if you want to enter you need to pass an identification test. Of course the country still practises that.
NB: text I wrote about visas and exhibiting in 1996:
http://conclusionism.com/dictionary/visa/visa_text_1996.html
In a way, those customs people do the same work as me.
They undress people from a different culture in order to find some evidence.
I am not negative about that, it's proof of a difference between me and them.

DF: I have visited a lot of borders recently. Everywhere at the frontier with the Schengen area, there are new, bigger, better, more secure check-points, either finished or in construction. Schengenland is just a word for you, so you don't think that something of the EU idea will be reality in future: hard external Visa borders and nearly no internal ones.

TG: I believe like you more that there will be hard external Visa borders but still hard to move around the EU. I don't see a kind of fluidity coming.
Especially from my point of location, Denmark.
But there are also borders between neighbours from the same street, due to the

general self-closing and fear of the other that the media and politicians like to establish. You can also observe (for example in France), cities having some kind of border rules about gipsy and other kinds of a non-wanted population in a local community. So every community starts to have exclusion rules, more or less on a small local scale, and exclusion systems in a legal or hidden way. (In Denmark for example, you can choose if you want a white or an ethnic taxi driver, as if to say a foreigner can have a working visa but people don't want to drive with him so it is a way of taking the working visa back.)

DF: Yes, that's also my observation, the illusion of a global "anything goes", and new local "exclusion rules". It was strange that I saw my first real "gated communities" in the flesh in Tallinn, Estonia last year. A really wealthy looking housing project, nice modern architecture, in the woods, just near the seaside, the beach with fences, surveillance cameras, closed gates and a sign/text: "photographing forbidden". First I was astonished, but then after having read about closed cities even during Russian times (like Liepaja in Latvia because of its important [war-] harbour), I imagined that the idea is maybe more familiar here. And maybe there are these international business people who do not know it any other way. You have made a lot of investigations into colonialism, tourism, immigration or cultural diversity, and you have worked for tv. Why can the media and the politicians affect people in that way you mention?

TG: When people are isolated from contact with ideas genuinely coming from different points of view (and not opinions from reading the media), they are more easy to manipulate, or order, they become perfect target groups for ideologies, products, politic as product ....
For politicians, paranoid and isolated people (because they are afraid of meeting anyone else apart from themselves) are perfect electors because politicians can offer them protection.
Everyone watching their media, faking speaking about the world. They watch all this and think alone, without sharing what they experience. Really, they watch in isolation, as if to say every one is open to everything in the world, on his private sofa. The sofa where nobody is welcome. (Scandinavian atmosphere to be precise.) Every body has a conscience of the other from his own sofa perspective, the sofa position is already a closed attitude. The sofa is a border.
The sofa formats the spirit. (With a tv position in front of the sofa distributing messages meant to scare people). No foreigners are invited onto those sofas. The borders are closed and the tv is telling us how the world opens up.

DF: "Sofa = the Scandinavian atmosphere" - what is an equivalent atmosphere in France then? And why was France such an important promoter of the EU process?

TG: I meant sofa-tv-loneliness during consumption of tv in Scandinavia. The tv entertainment is something that is watched alone (including the news) before bedtime. About France and EU, I don't have an expertise in that field.

DF: I think I understand, and I see that your "point of location" as you wrote before is Denmark, much of your work took place there, as well as elsewhere. The incident at Bergen airport is some time ago now. What was your latest encounter with borders, closed doors?

TG: My point of location is Denmark but also myself. It is difficult for me to see if, with time, borders are really becoming more difficult to pass, just as they are meant to be opening up, or if it is me who is changing. I can observe that with years passing, living in Denmark, I start to become like a Danish person. I am controlling my borders to strangers more, maybe it is also an effect of getting older in a western society, maybe it is the influence of the world situation that I perceive from the media, or maybe like I mention, it is because I am becoming more Danish. But any recent experience of mine that you are asking about is more an observation that myself, I am becoming a more closed and paranoid person. That is, from my point of observation, and this is a bit of a sad conclusion.

Indian Curry • Email interview with Ron Haselden (England-France)

Dear Ron, we first met in 1996. The EU (Schengen, Euro etc.) was just under construction. You invited me to visit Reading University - and you and Sharon already had the house in Brittany then. We did not talk much about that, but I thought of it more as a summer house. When we met this year in Bergen, I learned that for some years now, your son goes to school in France, so you are quite settled in Brittany. What was your first idea about buying a house in France and how did it change over the past years?

Ron Haselden: We used to go camping in France and somehow always ended up in a small campsite by the river Rance in Brittany. It was a simple and uncomplicated environment and sometimes I made small lead light sculptures there, soldering and lighting them from the car battery in the campsite. There was regular clientele who seemed to come each year and it was peaceful. It rained a lot and one day Sharon noticed that barns and old property was not expensive to buy and so we saw this as an opportunity to holiday somewhere dry and to make work in France. We bought a ruin and progressively improved it over the years. Francis, our son, was born here and with easy access to London via the ports and small airport, we managed to stay in France more often. I think we benefit from changing our environment between city and country life and if it was not still stimulating, we would go elsewhere. There are many interesting and serious writers and artists in Brittany, as well as good galleries and international events. The house is very, very old and that reinforces my attitude that we are only 'borrowing' it for a period of time in its history. Our histories are made up of ideas and that seems an interesting comparison with the aging stone and mortar.

DF: It's a very nice picture, your light sculptures on a campsite! Before I ask you more about your experiences working in public space, I would like to know how you experience the Channel. For me, it was, and maybe still is, a very strong border within Europe, not only physically but also politically between England and "the continent".

RH: Yes, the Channel is what you say it is; being British and living on a country separated by the sea from other lands contribute to the feeling that elsewhere is 'foreign' and away from home. It is odd for me to simply be able to walk into another country, like, say, between France and Germany, and within moments experience another language, another architecture, another cuisine and, in the past, another currency. The time delay for a British person makes 'going abroad' quite a time consuming affair even with Eurotunnel and convenient air travel. The moments of anticipation before stepping across that space are much extended. (They are mainly filled with waiting in lounges, experiencing bad and expensive coffee and being rigorously searched.) Nonetheless, it is always quite an occasion and somehow always more exciting because of this delay. When I return to London for periods of time, which I do frequently, I experience the very strong change in cultural atmosphere straight away, no matter where I have come from. It is hard to describe, but there is always a sense of energy and urgency in London, equal to none I experience elsewhere. It takes at least a day to get up to speed in London. The only place I felt this so strongly used to be in New York, but even there, it now seems to have calmed down and become less radical. Or more predictable, perhaps. It always seems a bonus to me that I am connected very strongly with my home country. I would never want to lose that and would never want to be an 'expat.' I wouldn't want my son to lose that either, but as a family we are perhaps now more 'European' than ever before.

DF: So maybe you are much more connected to, informed by and participating in the countryside life - the landscape, the people, the history - in France than you were in England as a Londoner. England is (like France) very much focused on the capital city. I realise that I was always being give an excuse by English people, especially artists, if they did not live in London. I remember seeing the very (sub-) urban light piece that you developed with the tenants of that big housing building, was it in North Kensington in London? How did your art projects in public space in France develop after your campsite installations?

RH: I have made several works in, or related to, my French experience. Fête, the big sound and light work, was stimulated by a visit to a local 'Fête du Blé' and after it was commissioned it was shown first in a country meadow at Feeringbury Manor in 1989. It went to the Serpentine Gallery and Canary Wharf in the UK before being erected by the roadside near our village of Plouër-sur-Rance in France. I have made videos in France and recently constructed two works for a brief period in my orchard and a field opposite the house. I am negotiating to make another work in a field this November. The work takes its immediate surroundings into account and at the same time I am not unaware of the strong political forces that exist in France within the agricultural communities. Nature does not sit idly being beautiful on its own. Neither should sculpture.

DF: With sculpture you are also occupying territory. Often - or is it always? - you need permission, which is sometimes a long procedure, I guess, everywhere. Have you noticed a different approach and different expectations from your side to this "occupation", either in your "home-country", England, or in your "second country", France - and in other foreign ones?

RH: My sculpture is usually temporary and I try to make work that causes the minimum of physical disturbance to the location in which it is made. In other words, it exists for a while and is removed, leaving the location unmolested. The request to whoever owns the space would therefore never seem very threatening. I try and involve that person or body in discussion beforehand and may even incorporate some ideas from them! It relies on people's memories and documentation for its continuing existence thereafter. In this sense, it relates to all the ingredients of its environment for the time that it is there. On works that do require permission for a permanent display, it is always sought by the agency that commissions it and France seems no different in this respect to anywhere else.

DF: You have just participated in the public event of "open studios" in the region of Britanny where you are living. Was it the first time you participated and what are your impressions and experiences?

RH: This is the first time I have participated in any 'open studio' event. Sharon also participated. It was an odd thing to do in such a rural environment, to allow the public to come and look at what you usually do in an atmosphere of privacy. Our visitors were never too numerous and I enjoyed the one-to-one discussions with people from all walks of life. None were artists. My neighbour, Marcelle Lemoine, told me to use her ground floor room. Normally, it's a store room with a 'terre battue' floor and was originally lived in by her mother-in-law. Marcelle laid a big log fire for me each day and I presented a trilogy of small lightworks with a sound-track, based on observation of my bees. The pieces were made specially for the show and in the atmosphere of such a strange and ancient room, they received much positive comment. Our friend, the artist, Marcel Dinahet, now wants to show the work in his studio in Rennes. It confirms my feelings that the more you explore ideas outside of mainstream art presentation, the more interesting it becomes.

DF: It's maybe possible to say, that your life is not only divided between two countries – England and France – but also between two life-styles -– the urban and the rural. How is your relation to Paris?

RH: I am travelling from Birmingham to London on a Virgin train as I write, with a visit to an opening at the Whitechapel Art Gallery on my arrival- then on to an Indian curry in one of my favourite restaurants with an old friend. – Paris?
Paris is not the most stimulating place I know. Nobody could say it is uninteresting, but three days seems to be the maximum time I need in Paris before I get itchy feet. This may be due to the fact that I have never given it a real chance. It always seems too beautiful and for some reason the art you see there always seems a bit behind the times and gives the impression that it's been somewhere else first. I never tire of London, London always grows on me. Paris is curious; perhaps it's not gritty enough for artists to flourish in at the moment.
Anywhere can change. It's the French art scene outside of Paris that seems more alive.

Dual Nationality · Email interview with Tanya Ury (England-Germany)

Dear Tanya, in 1992 you were showing your film "False Premises" and I was showing my photo installation "The Red Wig" at the 6th International Women Film Festival in Cologne. In 1994 you were there again with the programme "Don't call me erotic", you have moved to Cologne and since than we have contributed to each others projects. Did you move to Germany with the idea staying for such a long time?

Tanya Ury: In fact, I had already shown a previously made video, completed in Cologne, Incommunicado at the Feminale festival in 1990. As part of my Masters in Fine Art degree I was able to attend the Institute of Theatre, Film and Television Studies at the University of Cologne for a semester, with an Erasmus grant; more importantly I wished to continue my mature student investigations into the Shoah - the family had been dramatically affected by it and ultimately the Holocaust determined my preoccupations. My grandfather was still alive and I lived with him for some months on arriving in Cologne to make Incommunicado. It was not my first visit to Germany, but it was the first time I was making artwork about German-Jewish history, in Germany, which made absolute sense. My work was also later to strike a resonance with German spectators in a manner that I hadn't experienced in Britain; British viewers have often been perplexed or offended by the emotional and confrontational nature of some of my video work. In 1993 after making the performance/video Kölnisch Wasser in Cologne, I discovered that I felt more at home here than in the UK and moved within the same year. By the time I curated the opening programme 'Don't Call Me Erotic' in 1994 for the Feminale International Women's Film Festival, I had already decided to stay. The day before my performance all my worldly goods arrived by van in boxes, from the UK. With the video Hotel Chelsea – Köln 1995, people were often more interested in the erotic element of the Chelsea scenes than my reasons for making the art work, which was to understand better how the people of Cologne only 50 years before could simply ignore their Jewish neighbours, friends and lovers and let them go to their deaths without a word of protest.

DF: I am curious what the reason was that you "felt more at home here than in the UK"? It's not easy to imagine that German audience is open to be confronted with your work. What is the positive side of this confrontation and/or the negative?

TU: I don't know whether you have experienced the same phenomenon in Bergen, but sometimes when one is a stranger in a foreign land the locals can be especially generous and are more attentive. It is very pleasant to be on the receiving end of this shower of good will. Of course I have experienced anti-Semitism here but I have been witness to it outside Germany also. In Germany, because of the recent history, the issue of racism is taken very seriously – The Shoah and contemporary racism is a matter that is debated daily in the media. In England a very insidious kind of anti-Semitism is apparent; although there are far more Jewish citizens and therefore arguably more Jewish artists, the art is less readily exhibited, especially if it is Holocaust art; the English still fail to understand that the results of the Nazi acts of inhumanity were something that they are partially responsible for. Their main concern at the time was their island safety – the concept of making war did not include stopping the torture and mass murder in German concentration camps, which were never bomb targets. Now, possibly from a sense of shame, or denial, another kind of repression occurs when the type of confrontational Holocaust artwork I make is simply ignored. In the UK with the economic up turn of the nineties and the Brit Art pop culture, art that makes historical and social comment tends generally to be neglected.

DF: I guess one could pick up on a lot of the themes you have mentioned the Holocaust, racism, anti-Semitism, Jewish/German history etc. but I am interested in your choices or your preferences, the art work you made about Nazi-Gold, or the Hugo-Boss case, for instance.

TU: It is such a long time ago Doris, I can't remember exactly how the idea to have my body covered in gold leaf came about. I think it was a process of evolvement rather than sudden inspiration and was born out of Kölnisch Wasser

1993, body art observed through camera lens. Goldfinger was a film about Nazi gold. In having my own naked body re-covered with gold for the video/performance Golden Showers 1997, I hoped to demonstrate that a healing process may take place gradually (the covering took several hours). Each small square that the German art restorer Wolfgang Sassmanshausen carefully placed onto my oiled body created a protective layer, like a second skin but very fragile – as soon as I moved, cracks appeared in the facade. By making use of gold, I was obviously referring to the Nazi-gold scandals. But other elements were also suggested - the metaphors were mixed; an erotic constituent has often been present in my body art - hence the title Golden Showers, which describes urination as a sexual act. My interest in Hugo Boss was awakened in 1998, when my brother told me he had heard of their fascist past. But it wasn't till January 2000, when a friend gave me a newspaper article about Dr. Elisabeth Timm's research into the Boss history, that I started to engage with the subject. I chose the Boss story, although many other German companies profited during the war years by exploitation, because Boss was a clothing manufacturer; the notion that dressing also encompasses the component of disguise, intrigued me. Hugo Ferdinand Boss' company made gentleman's suits in Metzingen, until 1931. Later, as a Nazi party member, his firm made uniforms, employing a slave labour force that will probably never receive compensation. Today the privatised fashion empire creates contemporary fashion with conformingly uniform designs.

If I am perfectly honest, my taking on various protective mantles is not just about awareness of social responsibility but is also about ad-dressing personal wounds: I was maltreated as a child. When I was 24 I was scalded on a train in England: a third of my body received third degree burns, which turned septic after a laundry strike in the hospital. I only recovered after getting skin grafts. As an adult I again suffered domestic violence within marriage and experienced another kind of violence when a botched surgical contraceptive procedure caused infection and infertility. To correspond with the clothing metaphor I am coming out of the closet here. Some of the brutal encounters were accidental, but I am sure the family dysfunction, has a lot to do with the lived and genetic memory of pogrom, and Diaspora.

DF: I am jumping now a bit, there is a lot to discuss, but limited time and space, so I would like to come back to the topic of crossing borders, nations and nationalities. You have dual nationality and you also took this theme up in one of your pieces. I think it's not easy to get dual nationality in Germany? Today or for the future do you have dreams or wishes to move back to England or somewhere else?

TU: In Germany, correct me if I'm wrong Doris, because the laws keep changing, children may have dual nationality, that is German nationality and that of their non-German parents', until the offspring are 18 years old; then they have to choose between one or the other. The regulations for adults originating from another land are always draconian – they don't have the child's privilege of choice (I took the subject up in the art work Dual(national)ity, 2000).

My parents were both German but I was not required to surrender my English nationality when I acquired German citizenship in 1992, probably because of our special history; the photocopies of my mother's first German passport that I brought to the German embassy in London, as evidence of her nationality, displayed the swastika stamp - on my father's birth certificate furthermore, the name Israel was added to his given name Hans-Peter.

On re-checking my documents, I just discovered a German embassy communication, which I hadn't bothered to read at the time, informing that if it came to requiring diplomatic protection from one country, I would, after all, have to forego citizenship of the other.

Actually having German nationality has afforded me no advantages per se; I acquired it on principle, so to speak. It was a 'statement' along with all my other art activities and was ultimately about coming to terms with the 'German' side of my identity, although it upset my mother at the time. But my grandmother's words of advice to me in childhood, demonstrating the fugitive mentality that is my heritage, were: "Several passports are better than one, for you never know..."

I never met my father's parents Ury and Ullmann from Ulm, who fell victim to the

Nazis. I have no sense of loyalty, any nationalistic feelings or nostalgia towards one or another place. One great-grandmother came from Russia; England was just another stop en route. I am where I am, because of the Jewish Diaspora, no more and no less.
Although I make efforts to maintain contacts, I have only been able to show my work in the UK twice in the last six years. This has led to a certain sense of resentment. I was born, studied and spent 41 years of my life in England and would like to show the work that I make here, over there.
As far as moving away from Germany, who knows where future paths will lead ... I remain open.

Northern Souls · Email interview with Anu Vahtra (Estonia-Norway)

Dear Anu, we met at Kunsthøgskolen in Bergen in Norway this year, and when I got to know that an Estonian student was to join our department, I contacted you to ask if you could look for some old postcards from borders and shores in the Baltic States. I was already working on my Retour project and had visited Estonia, Latvia and Lithuania a year ago but forgot to look for postcards for this publication. You then came in the middle of the Nordic winter to Bergen and you did bring postcards. Some I am now using in this publication. Why did you choose Bergen for your exchange studies?

Anu Vahtra: Until I applied for the scholarship in KHiB, I didn't consider coming to Norway at all. Somehow I didn't pay attention to this country before, I'd been always looking in some other direction. Of course, I've heard about the nature of this country but I guess I never felt wealthy enough to go travelling there. Once I saw the note about the opportunity to study in Bergen, I thought why not try and go to a place of which even the idea was new for me. My professor here told me about the school. In her opinion, the photography department is high level over there and known for its international staff, so the choice was made. It was sort of random, though after applying, I didn't consider going to any other country any more.

DF: So you didn't have any previous experience about the country, the people etc. Do you remember your first days in Norway? What made a deep impression on you?

AV: Yes, of course I remember my first day in Norway. I was a little confused, leaving Estonia came sort of suddenly and I didn't realise it before I arrived in Bergen. I was really impressed by the kindness of people. My aunt had organised one of her friends to pick me up at the airport; having somebody welcoming me there made me feel much more comfortable. Thanks to his example, it seemed that all the Norwegian people must be as nice and friendly as he was. And nobody disappointed me afterwards. The weather was also something that caught my attention. I came from snowy Tallinn, also Oslo was in deep snow, but Bergen welcomed me with strong rain and fog. The fog was in fact so thick that it was hard to understand what the new surroundings were like.

DF: Did the fog clear later? And you came in contact with your fellow art students and their work, their way of working, their concerns?

AV: It all cleared up. I was able to see quite soon where I was going to spend the next 5 months. Coming into contact with the people around me took me a little more time. I think the myth about northern people has some truth in it. And as I'm from north as well, in a way there was a double effect. First there's kind of a wall around them, but after some time it'll melt and you'll find incredibly warm and lovely people inside. It was very interesting for me to see how people work. I've been stuck in one school system during my whole studying period, so it was very refreshing to meet students' open-mindedness and independence in the work process.

DF: The art scene is often seen and categorised as rooted in certain national boundaries: British (yBa), German (painting), German (photography), Finnish (photography), Italian (Arte Povera) etc. Did you learn

something about your Estonian/ East European identity by having a physical distance to your country?

AV: I think the art scene in Estonia is very fragmentised. It's hard to define the identity through one field, it might be possible when considering the general theme or direction. The Soviet period has its role here; in contemporary society, 10 years of independence is a bit too short a time to search for and actually find one's identity. The art scene has of course existed for more than the last decade, but it's hard to deal with different influences. The artists are individuals, their questions about their identity also individual. Being away from Estonia made me think about my belonging. It was hard to identify myself in Norway, it felt like being lost, I couldn't find a starting point. So I started my work at a new point for me, with new tools and with no connections to my previous work. I was hoping it might help me to find some confidence.

DF: I was also thinking of the term "Baltic Photography", that also appeared in exhibitions/catalogues some years ago. Does this mean anything to you?

AV: Considering the number of the countries that belong to the Baltic Sea region, "Baltic Photography" is a rather wide term. I think the photography that fits under this "title" is as diverse as it would be on any occasion when artworks with different backgrounds are placed side by side and defined as one group. The 3rd Ars Baltica Triennal of Photographic Art which at the moment is being exhibited here in Tallinn, is not a very good example of an exhibition, though under one title one can see as many different approaches as there are artists. Lately I have discovered photographers that are interesting for me among young Finnish and Lithuanian artists.

DF: During your time in Bergen, you were quite successfully productive in your work. Did you show your work to people in Tallinn? Do you have future plans to work somewhere else, and if so, why?

AV: Yes, I made a presentation the next week after coming back. Although quite a few people showed up, they weren't very generous in giving feedback and criticism. In fact, I don't know what the expectations were, but generally my professor was satisfied with my work. Though I'd like to discuss it more thoroughly and with more people. Hopefully I can do so in the beginning of the coming semester. For the future, I have no certain plans yet, but definitely after a while I want to work somewhere else again. It's important to keep your mind fresh and leaving the country of origin is one way to do that. Hopefully I'll be able to do my master's degree abroad. Who knows, I might return to Bergen - Vilde mentioned that I'm welcome to work as a guest artist at Isotop.

DF: Norway is not an EU country. Do you remember 1st May 2004, the EU celebration day for its new member states? Did you miss not being in your home country to join in, in whatever way, this important political event? And later on that month, do you remember the Norwegian National Day on 17th May?

AV: 1st May was quite a random day. For me, Estonia becoming a member of the EU was not an event worth celebrating. I'm quite sceptical towards it, it's not just to do with economic wellbeing like it was talked up to be. Of course I understand that there are two sides to belonging to the union, but this especially is why there's nothing to celebrate. So I was rather pleased that I could spend the day outside of the EU. 17th May (Norwegian National Day of Independence) I'm going to remember for a very long time. Until this day, I had an impression that people in Norway are very calm, keeping their emotions always under control, but this day ruined the impression completely. I guess all the citizens were on the streets and despite the rain, people were in a gushingly good mood. Norwegians seem to be very proud of their nationality and they are not ashamed to express it publicly. And probably they are also proud of not being a member of the EU.

DF: Have there been occasions when you have been desperately homesick?

AV: No, I have never felt that feeling. At least, not in such a radical way. Sometimes while I was in Norway, I did think about how it would be to go back home. I was curious, but that was it. I felt at home in Norway, living and working there seemed to be so natural that it was quite hard to leave. Though I often thought of my friends back in Estonia, not longing for them, but rather wanting to share moments and experiences with them. There was a lot worth sharing.

Nostalgia of Origin • Email interview with Dan Mihaltianu (Romania-Germany)

Dear Dan, in 1996, we were in the same exhibition at Schloß Plüschow in North-East Germany. As far as I remember, you came from Berlin then. We are now teaching in the same Department at Kunsthøgskolen in Bergen, and you are still living in Berlin. You are from Bucharest, Romania - when and how did your move from Bucharest to Berlin begin?

Dan Mihaltianu: I came to Berlin in 1993 as artist in residence at Künstlerhaus Bethanien. After one year in Bethanien, I got a studio in a squatted building in Mitte. This way, Berlin became my first address and Bucharest the second one. I still have an apartment and studio there.
In this respect, the "move" to Berlin came as natural, with no "breaking off", and I had the freedom to return at any moment to my home town.

DF: I guess that to move back and forth from Berlin to Bucharest was also possible because of the changes since 1989. At this time, Germany was very focused on East Germany. How was the situation in Bucharest and Romania for you?

DM: If you mean the situation in Romania before 1989, then this is a long story. It was the most violent collapse of communism in the Eastern Bloc. The reason is that all the liberal reforms implemented by Gorbachev in the Soviet Union, and similar ones in most of the other countries of the system, were not taking place in Romania. The Eighties were the most difficult years in the post war history of Romania. Ceausescu was politically isolated abroad, the economy was almost collapsing and the national communist propaganda was exacerbated. In this situation, culture was considered to be part of the propaganda and everything that didn't serve those purposes was simply ignored by the regime. On top of all this, corruption was institutionalized. Corruption seems to be a Byzantine heritage which can be adjusted to any political system in Romania. But at that time, corruption also had a "positive" aspect: almost everything was possible if you knew the right people or had enough money. In terms of art, not so much was going on. Apart from official exhibitions, meant to celebrate the Ceausescu Regime, only a few group or individual shows could be considered as interesting. Even less numerous were the underground events and the audience was very limited. In this respect, the artists were divided into three categories: the ones who were involved in the official art, others who were developing a parallel personal discourse, and many who were practising a "double-face" attitude in order to survive politically and financially. The "double moral" was, and still is, a kind of national sport.

DF: What about your own strategy?

DM: My strategy at that time was close to the second position described above. In the period between 1978 and 1989, I developed a large body of work which was shown partially in difficult conditions in Romania. Parallel to this, I was participating in international shows mainly with graphics, photographs and experimental works. This action was limited by the postal and Customs regulations and the fact that there was no direct contact with the people organizing those events. In these conditions, a large part of my work was not presented to the public and is still not known to the art world.

DF: According to what I read recently in the Magazine "ART", you are going to participate in a show that is opening the Ceausescu Palace in Bucharest as a museum. How is the discussion and situation nowadays?

Could you think of showing your early pieces there now?

DM: I will participate with a new work in the inaugural show at the National Museum of Contemporary Art in Bucharest. I don't know if I will ever show one of my early works in this place because it is not clear yet what the profile and the strategy of the institution are. Until now, there was no special interest in rediscovering the relatively recent art history of Romania. Further, the whole event is a kind of "adventure" of which nobody knows how long it is going to last.
A short review of the history of the place and the circumstances in which the museum will open could be instructive. The building known abroad as the "Ceausescus' Palace" was built with the idea of hosting all the institutions of the Socialist Republic of Romania. The architectural complex called the "Civic Centre", which includes the palace, the boulevard and a large surrounding area, was not entirely finished in 1989.
Even today numerous buildings are still in the early stages of construction, while others were finished in a different way to originally planed. The "People's House", the "House of the Republic" or the "Palace of the Parliament", which is the latest official name, is the second largest office building in the world after the Pentagon. The Parliament moved there after 1989 but uses only one wing of the building. The rest is partially open to the public and has become the best tourist attraction. Certain rooms can be rented for special occasions such as weddings, parties and other events. The interiors are frequently used as settings for international film productions.
The National Museum of Contemporary Art will be installed in one of the back wings of the building. It is a relatively small part of the building, but taking into consideration the proportions of the whole, it will be one of the largest museums in Europe. This mixture of institutions, combining politics, business, culture and entertainment, is not just a local curiosity but part of a global phenomenon called "Disneylandisation".

DF: What are the main arguments around the plan to locate the Museum of Contemporary Art in the old communist "Palace of the Parliament"?

DM: The controversial debates around MNAC (Muzeul National de Arta Contemporana), which have not only national but also international echoes, revolve around these issues:
- The location, the symbolism, the size and the function of the building (the Parliament) are considered to be inappropriate for a contemporary art museum.
- The implication of the Government in the foundation and the "affaires" of the museum. - The decision of the Prime Minister, who considers himself an art collector, and supporter of arts, that the museum should open in this building is believed to have political consequences, especially for the presidential elections.
- The appointed leadership of the museum is not considered to be the best choice for such an important art institution, because of its relation to "political power" and its incapacity to fairly represent all the groups and interests of either the Romanian or the - why not? -international art scene.
- The conflict between different fractions and groups of artists, who have opposing opinions and interests regarding a contemporary national museum, is sharpening in the months before the official opening. The group of "older and more traditional" artists is afraid that it will be excluded because of the orientation towards experimental art and new media. A group of "socially involved" artists are using their opposition as an "artistic weapon" in an attempt to gain attention at home and abroad.

DF: How do the international people try to step into the process?

DM: Many international curators, museum directors and artists seem to be interested in what is going on around the new museum. The main attraction is the building itself rather than the Romanian art scene. Then there is the challenge of a new "zone of influence" waiting to be conquered, but of course everybody is very careful. What almost everybody seems to forget is the fact that a museum is an institution built for the future, regardless of who the founders are, or the first directors, the first artists or art works to be shown.

DF: So, it could be quite important to be present in Bucharest during these times. I guess you keep up contact with a lot of places and people ... by e-mail? What do you think about the notions of exile, nomad, migrant, or jet-set even, that have turned up in the discourse around artistic practice over the last few years?

DM: Email is the usual way to keep in contact with Bucharest but I also spend at least two months there every year. I also meet more and more Romanian friends outside the country in different exhibitions and at other artistic events. I think jet nomadism is the most appropriate term to describe my situation and the artistic praxis related to mobility. To my opinion exile and migration are terms that don't apply anymore to the European region at least in terms of art. Half of the former Eastern Europe is part of the EU and the rest will join it soon. In this respect "the globalization makes the exile non relevant, what remains is the nostalgia of origins".

DF: Nomads, jet or otherwise, are normally not alone but belong to tribes, families, communities - groups based on old, sometimes traditional and very strong relations, even dependencies. I wonder how this feels nowadays, with so-called jet-nomadism and networks. And how stable or fragile this all may be?

DM: The same rules do not necessarily apply to the term "nomadism" in art as they do to the social phenomenon of nomadism. In this respect, "Art Nomadism" is not a mass phenomenon. Artists are individualists. If they belong to a group or community, they feel free to develop new networks and connect to other cultural structures than the ones they originally come from.
At the same time, "nomads" as an artistic issue could also be well used by artists who are not necessarily in a nomadic position. Despite the idealistic ideas of "artistic freedom", the art scene is divided into "zones of interest". What we can see very well at the European level, but which could also be applied to other areas, is the fact that the division is still the rule of the game. "Western European Artist", "Central European Artist", "Balkan Artist", "Baltic Artist", "Post Soviet Artist" etc. are "labels" that most of the artists have to stick on according to their origins, in order to survive.

DF: The good things with these "labels" is perhaps that work is not seen completely out of autobiographical and historical context – certain political and social circumstances create certain expressions of content and form – as long as diversity is still included.
Do you have any idea what would happen if not only the artists, but also the institutions might start to become mobile – not only one or two of them like Manifesta, but many?

DM: The mobility in terms of institutions is not an unusual phenomenon in our days. Not only, financial, economical, social, religious or political but also cultural institutions are spreading around the world. Of course there are different levels of mobility and different kind of interest according to nature of each institution. Almost every country has a foreign cultural institute, like Goethe Institute or British Council, which operates abroad. Some of them are taking an active role in the local cultures where they are present, according to the strategies of the governments they belong. But, they don't have the freedom to act independently. There are institutions like "Open Society" for example, that are no longer acting in the name of a state or government but in individual, group or corporate interests. Despite the "openness" they still have an ideology to follow for example neo liberalism.

DF: What about the art institutions?

DM: Coming back to Museums, Galleries and Biennials, they are also having dependencies in different continents, countries or cities: Guggenheim New York, Guggenheim Bilbao, Guggenheim Berlin, Ludwig Museum Cologne, Muzeum Ludwig Budapest, and so on. Of course the biennials are connected to a specific place like Venice or Sao Paolo but what is mobile is the idea of a biennial, which is spreading across continents from Moscow to Busan, from Istanbul to Tirana.

But the real "nomads" are the directors and the curators. They just move from one institution to another as soon they use up the local resources or finish their contracts and take their artists with them. What we are seeing in all the contemporary art events around the world are curators and artists belonging to an international network that applies to the same rules as the "corporate capitalism": money, power and domination. The "democratization of art", which is the motto, seems to be just a cynic concept: "everybody could be an artist" and "everybody has the right to be famous for five minutes". The ones who circulates those ideas make sure first they are artists and famous for more then just five minutes, if not forever.

Two Cities • Email interview with Maja Bajevic (Bosnia and Herzegovina-France)

Dear Maja, we met in a bar after your lecture at the Academy in Bergen. I guess this was just one of many journeys that you have made over the last few years in order to show and present your work: The Netherlands, Poland, USA and Germany are just some stops I remember. And I recently saw your work "Women at Work - Under Construction" in Leipzig, Germany. And of course, shows in Paris and Sarajevo. In your biography, it always says "Maja Bajevic (Sarajevo/Paris)" and the work I have seen in Leipzig is site-specific to Sarajevo. How have you moved and worked between these two different cities, cultures and languages over the years? Was there a crucial episode that influenced your decision to move to Paris?

Maja Bajevic: In 1989, I was in Paris over the summer and saw an exhibition that impressed me very much "Les Magiciens de la Terre". So, later, in 1991 I came to Paris to study. I had a scholarship for eight months or one school year. In April 1992, the war started in my country (ex-Yugoslavia) and I could not go back. So instead of 8 months, I stayed 8 years in a row, then went back to Sarajevo for two and a half years, afterwards went to Zurich for a 6 month residency and then back to Paris again. I think that the Sarajevo/Paris part of my biography is completely correct – these are the two cities that have formed me, although they are not the only ones I have lived in. As a child I lived in Munich for 6 years, then in Zurich... But it seems that these are the only two cities I tend to come back to, and if home could be defined as a place you come back to, then I guess for me it would be Sarajevo/Paris.

DF: So from an early age, you changed city and country quite often and you also had to adjust to cultural diversity, foreign mentality and politics. Both Sarajevo and Paris are capital cities – of Bosnia and Herzegovina and of France. When you write that these two cities have "formed" you, I am interested in how this is connected to the city itself, and how much, and in which way, to the nation, i.e. the national politics, the society's mentality, art and culture.

MB: I think it is more the cities themselves then nations. We always hear people say that New York is great but New York is not America. I think that goes also for Paris and for Sarajevo. As for mentality, I think that in that concern, I am really lucky to live in two cities. I recognize their mutual mentality, clearly, but do not have to participate in it.
And art - my choice to live in a big city, a metropolis, was connected to the desire to see a lot of art. In Paris, you can really see almost everything that is interesting in the world at the moment. In Sarajevo, it's different, there I am more taking part in the "making of art", so again it seems that I need both influences.

DF: Can you give some insight in what you mean by "... more taking part in the making of art" in Sarajevo?

MB: Well, Sarajevo was a very open city after the war. It seemed as if all the laws were broken, all the history gone and everything seemed possible. It was important to re-conquer the city, to do things in public spaces, to give public space back its function - under grenades, a public space is hardly public anymore. Luckily the city authorities were not against the art in the streets. Maybe because they did not pay

attention, there were more urgent problems, but this kind of freedom in the time lapse between the ultimate out-of-the ordinary, which is war, and the ordinary, was very fruitful for a whole generation of artists.

DF: With your biography, does the process/progress of the European Union have any meaning or impact on your living and/or working conditions?

MB: Unfortunately Bosnia and Herzegovina is not amongst the "chosen ones" from Eastern European countries. That is really sad, especially because the ex-Yugoslavia was, before the war, by far the most developed and open of the Eastern European countries, and we, ex-Yugoslavs, considered ourselves deeply European. Now the EU army is in Bosnia, but Bosnia is not in the EU. I have a double Bosnian/French nationality, so it does not affect my life in that way any more, but my artist colleagues from Sarajevo have to ask for a Visa to travel to each exhibition in which they participate abroad and that makes their life extremely complicated. What hurts me a lot is also the abbreviation that is very much in use, when people say the EU and take it to mean Europe, forgetting that Europe is before anything else a geographical, then a historical and then also a culture-logical fact that can not be changed in accordance with the politics of today. The European Union is a very recent fact compared to ancient Greece, Rome, the Ottoman and Austro-Hungarian Empire, and all of that was, and is, Europe. A bit more to the east, though.

DF: Creativity in European states was often connected to identity, and art to a certain notion of nation, nationality and its cultural tradition. Art is/was an export article, like yBa, German Painting, Nordic Miracle, Italian Transavanguardia. How do you react to the notion of Balkan Art? And what do such categories mean today for cross-border, migrant, diaspora, for nomadic ways of working and living?

MB: If you mean the series of exhibitions made on Balkan Art, I think it is a good thing, since we are still in this nation-state, nation-arts system. Especially since they were done by really great curators (Harald Szeemann, René Block) which is not always the case with national or regional exhibitions, so it is rather flattering for the art and the artists from the region. There were some very young Kurdish artists in the exhibitions that had never even left their country before, and who are great artists; that is the most beautiful thing about it. Now, if we talk about the system as such, I think it is rather restrictive. I always prefer exhibitions that are not based on a national or regional basis. But if you think about it a bit deeper, it is just a reflection of the political and economic reality we live in. The British council supports British artists, AFAA supports French artists etc. so for any institution that organizes exhibitions, it is much easier to work with Western European, American, or Japanese artists since the countries they come from will support the project financially. That is maybe why there are more of these artists around. I do not think it is a question of artistic quality - on the contrary, the most interesting artists, from my point of view, come from other parts of the world, but the market and art history are still dominated by the ones who have a strong financial background. Being a nomad also means being on your own, which has its good and bad sides.

DF: Nomads also belong to tribes, families, communities - groups based on old, sometimes traditional or very strong relations, even dependencies. I wonder how this feels nowadays, with "nomadism" and networks replacing such structures? And how stable or fragile all this may be?

MB: Well there is a nomadic art community, you could probably also call it family or tribe, that does rely on strong relations and dependencies, as you have put it. The laws have maybe changed a bit from the ancient nomadic laws and rules but new rules have replaced old ones. One is either 'in' or 'out of the system. Another thing are the networks that one creates on a more private, intimate basis and these networks tend to be more reliable, from my point of view, then any system can be. And if you are talking about people that have, out of one reason or another, moved, then I don't think that they can be regarded as nomadic, but rather as migratory.

Web-cam photographs

On the border to Russia
Stills from DVD slide show, 10 mins, 2003/2005

Vaalimaa, Rekkaparkki [225]
Vaalimaa [226]
Nuijamaa [227]
Imatra [228]
Niirala [229]
Vartius [230]

MAERSK

Is there nothing else to absorb us? Nothing apart from the chic clothes, the immaculate street scene, the surplus of income and the countless ways of slaying boredom, if this too is bestowed upon us? Should our longings restrict themselves to the doctrines of salvation of the balanced gross domestic products from Kiev to Lisbon? Where we once were, must you now be – but do you want to be us? That is the question.
© Stasiuk, Andrzej, "View onto a soft, painless extermination", Süddeutsche Zeitung, 30.04.2004

"Schengen" is the name given to the common external border of the continental members of the EU, and to the absence of border controls among them. The former was a logical consequence of the latter. The intention of the French, German, Belgian, Luxembourgeois, and Dutch governments who signed the original Schengen treaty in 1985 was not to create an external border, but to remove border controls among themselves. They meant to set a good example for other European Community (EC) members by fulfilling one of the main aspirations of European integration, the free movement of people. Although they rightly anticipated that west European citizens would favor easy movement for themselves, they also understood that state borders play an enormously important psychological function in west European societies. These governments understood that west Europeans deprived of the sense of security arising from national borders would have to be "compensated" by the creation of an external frontier comprising all participating states. As the Schengen zone grew to include all of the continental members of the EU, and was incorporated into the EU's institutions, the coupling of the removal of internal borders with a strengthened common external border was unquestioned by all participants. For two major reasons, allowing the unhindered movement of people within the EU has unintended consequences quite distinct from allowing the free movement of goods. First, although Schengen (like European integration in general) began as an elite project, it is one of the few EU initiatives that harmonizes with public opinion. Once in place, both internal freedom of movement and the hard external frontier became untouchable at the level of the domestic politics of participating states. Second, more than other projects of European integration, the creation of an external frontier directly requires the EU to take on state-like functions, assume state-like roles, and acquire state-like capacities. The theories of European integration held by most European elites contend that the creation of European political structures will emerge from governmental cooperation, social interaction, or economic integration. Border control is the unplanned but irresistible shortcut: It is the policy that demands that the EU behave like a territorial state.
© Snyder, Timothy, "The Wall around the West", Eurozine, 06.01.2005

The tunnel is grossly underused. Some 150,000 trains pass through the tunnel every year out of a capacity of 300,000 while Britain's domestic railway network is crammed with traffic.
© Clark, Andrew, "Stuck in the tunnel", The Guardian, 25.10.2003

The situation is gloomy. Eurotunnel, the operator of the rail connection under the Channel, is complaining of an annual loss of £1.3 billion. The operating profit of £170 million was utterly wiped out by the burden of interest. [...] "If we had known ten years ago that the passenger and freight revenue was to be so small, then we would never have built the Tunnel." (Eurotunnel boss R. Shirref)
© "Eurotunnel: miscalculates", DIE ZEIT, 12.02.2004

In the years that have passed since the ending of the Cold War, Russia, Norway and NATO have severely reduced their military presence in the Arctic North. However, through its energy reserves and nuclear waste, the region is of continuing strategic significance. Furthermore, the conflict between Russia and Norway in the Barents Sea over the boundaries of the trade zone – the biggest remaining border conflict in Europe – still remains unresolved, despite the two making gentle inroads towards coming together.
© von Lucius, Robert, "Concerns about the Barents Sea", FAZ, 03.06.2004

Approximately 80 percent of vehicles crossing Poland's eastern border in 2002 carried some goods for sale. Even family visits were often combined with petty trade activity, providing a much-needed boost to the local economies, which is particularly important because Poland's east is the poorest part of the country and will constitute the poorest region in the enlarged EU. At the same time, the western regions of Ukraine and Belarus, while the most prosperous in those countries, are still much poorer.
In 2002, Ukrainians crossed the border 6 million times, Belarusians and Russians 4 million times each. The total value of cross-border trade amounted to about $7 billion. While this accounts for only about 10 percent of the total trade for Poland, it is nonetheless crucial to the economy of eastern Poland and even more vital to the economies of western Ukraine and Belarus.
In October 2003, Poland imposed full EU border controls and began demanding visas from its neighbors in accordance with the Schengen requirements. In order to smooth the transition, Poland has offered free or greatly discounted visas. Despite this effort, the immediate effect of the new restrictions was staggering: According to some estimates, crossings at border points fell by more than two-thirds. Although the figures may rise in the future, as more citizens acquire multiple-entry visas, the border restrictions will make their presence felt in the short run.
© Jacuch, Radoslaw, "EU: The Curtain Drops", Transitions Online, 20.05.2004

There are currently three so-called "Euroregions" on Poland's eastern frontier: The Niemen Euroregion (between Poland, Lithuania, Russia, and Belarus); the Bug Euroregion (on the Polish-Ukrainian border); and the Carpathian Euroregion (between Poland, Ukraine, Hungary, Slovakia, and Romania).
© Jacuch, Radoslaw, "EU: The Curtain Drops", Transitions Online, 20.05.2004

Marijampole (Lithuania) is where the streams of traffic going south from Helsinki, St. Petersburg, Tallin, Riga and Kaunas, towards Warsaw, Lodz, Prague and Budapest; or west, towards Posen, Berlin and Western Europe meet together with those that lead from the Baltic coast towards inland Russia, to the Black Sea and to Central

Asia: from Kaliningrad to Vilnius, Minsk, Moscow, Kiev, Odessa, Astrakhan, Alma-Ata. For a decade, the whole of west Europe has been delivering its cars – used motors of all vintages and categories – to Marijampole, and the whole of east Europe has stocked up with cars at this bazaar. Marijampole is a centre of east European modernisation, which was first mobilised through cars and in some zones still is.
© Schlögel, Karl, "Europe's Comeback", Lettre International, Spring 2004

Although cross-border traffic picked up a little in the latter half of October and has continued to rise, it was still a far cry from the days before European Union regulations prompted Poland to change its open-border policy with Ukraine. According to customs officials, somewhere between 7,000 and 10,000 Ukrainians used to cross into Poland every day at the Shegini-Medyka checkpoint alone. Their numbers have now dwindled to a mere 2,000 a day. Traffic has followed the same pattern at the Krakovets-Korchova border checkpoint: 8,000 used to cross each day, but now the figure is just 1,600.
Where have the Ukrainians who earlier besieged border crossings gone? Most of them are now besieging the Polish consulates in Kiev, Lutsk, Odessa, and, above all, in Lviv. If, in the first days of the new border-crossing procedure, the queue of visa seekers at the Lviv consulate numbered 200 to 300, it soon rocketed to some 3,000. Since it can take days to get from the back to the front of the queue, the names are put on a list and applicants told to come back at fixed times for a roll call. The rules are tough: no-shows or latecomers are sent packing. At the moment, it can be a good two weeks before applicants come face to face with a consular official.
© Fediv, Lesya, "Pole-Axed", Transitions Online, 30.01.2004

Expansion towards the east stood right at the beginning of European history, thousands of years ago. It began with the violent Germanisation of Slavic tribes but it did not stop at bloody subjugation. Clearances and town developments, settlers from all over the whole of west Europe, the settlers' right that a Polish prince drew up, the technical 'know-how' from the harrow to the scythe, from the iron plough to double-entry bookkeeping – this entire transfer integrated the east into the world economy of the time. The big wave of Christianisation – it too accompanied by terror and the sword – nevertheless brought an admission into the expanding cultural community at the same time. Fear of conquest by the Turks finally became the enduring binding force.
© Schmidt-Häuer, Christian, "At the lower end of the spiral of chance", DIE ZEIT, 29.04.2004

Since time immemorial, the Adriatic has been a border region and transit zone. Over centuries, the Ottoman and Venetian fleets competed here for maritime supremacy, and Christian pirates (Uskok) from Dalmatia and Muslim freebooters from Ulcinj in Montenegro fought with one another. Towards the end of the 15th century, thousands of Albanians fled from the Ottoman's conquering campaign to Italy. There are still Albanian speaking villages in Calabria, Sicily and Basilicata today.
© Dérens, Jean Arnault, "Seafarers without ships – The Adriatic, a European inland sea", Le monde diplomatique, 09.07.2004

Characters in Joseph Roth's fiction roamed the length and breadth of Central Europe paying little heed to boundaries. In his works, set in the twilight of the Habsburg Empire, the sole border of the kind we think of today - impenetrable to those lacking the proper documents - was just a few miles from the writer's birthplace, the frontier between Austria-Hungary and the Russian Empire in eastern Galicia, today in Ukraine. Prior to World War I, it was easy to travel from Sarajevo and Trieste in the south to Danzig (Gdansk) and Koenigsberg (Kaliningrad) in the north, from Strassburg (Strasbourg) and Cologne in the west to Czernowits (Chernivtsi) and Lwow (Lviv) in the east. In this region of the Old Continent, the institution of the passport was virtually unknown before 1918. The same was true of the British Empire and the United States, but where exchange of goods and ideas as well as free travel within the Anglo-Saxon world have never been seriously hampered by borders or decrees, in Central Europe, restrictions replaced this freedom of movement overnight with the creation of numerous ethnic nation states and the Soviet Union, all built on the ruins of the former, much more permissive empires. Since that time, the passport and the visa have been deified. Possessing a passport or visa issued by a Western state meant it was possible to escape the Holocaust or Soviet repressions. Foreign travel became a strictly limited good. Passports and jealously guarded borders are a badge of modernity enshrined in the form of the nation state. After the collapse and breakup of the Soviet bloc, the hope was that not only would communist restrictions on freedom of travel be removed, but also that borders would be relegated to where they belong - on maps. In much of Western Europe, a semblance of what Central Europeans enjoyed prior to 1914 was created during the 1980s and 1990s when the Schengen Agreement came into force. The main foundation of this new order is the freedom of movement of persons unhindered by any border checks.
© Kamusella, Tomasz, "Borderlands: Beyond the Pale?", Transitions Online, 11.02.2005

Even so, hostile and bigoted reporting continues, with casual disregard for any distinction between asylum seeker, refugee, failed asylum seeker or economic migrant. In most articles, the terms are used randomly, as if synonymous. In the Daily Mail, Ross Benson has been running a series of stories about the Roma, warning of an invasion of Gypsies once the European Union is enlarged in May. The Roma, it is widely agreed, remain the most disliked and despised of all European ethnic minorities. In January 2004, the Sunday Times took up the theme, suggesting that up to 100,000 Roma were on their way. The next day, the Sun added that after three months in the UK, these Roma would be "entitled to health, education, pension and welfare benefits". The Daily Express then inflated the figure to 1.6 million: "Gypsies prepare to invade Britain". Though two days later they amended this figure to 40,000, they predicted an "economic disaster" just the same. Even The Economist spoke of the "coming hordes". On 22 January, the Mail front page covered a report by the Organisation for Economic Co-operation and Development, saying that Britain, which was taking one in five of the Western world's asylum seekers, had "failed to turn the asylum tide". The article, it later turned out, was based on figures from 2002, and ignored the fact that the UK is currently eighth in the immigration league tables relative to size of population, well behind Austria, Norway, Sweden, Switzerland and Ireland. In any case, under EU agreements, old EU members may keep their labour markets closed to new entrants for a transition period of seven years, and research has already shown that the desire to move to the West from the countries joining in May may not

be all that high. Lies, inaccuracies, exaggerations, untruths: this is the climate in which the current asylum world lives, in which policy is made not so much on evidence as in response to media and public perception, and in which those seeking asylum, buffeted by the chaotic, contradictory and discriminatory asylum procedures now operating across the Western world, scramble for a toehold using any method they can. Not long ago, Kofi Annan, secretary general of the United Nations, told the European Parliament that Europe's anti-immigration rhetoric was "de-humanising" people. "This silent human rights crisis" he went on, 'shames our world."
© Moorehead, Caroline, "Necessary lies", Eurozine:Index on Censorship, 03.05.2004

The EU has always taken an ambiguous stance toward the situation of the Eastern and Central European Roma. It advocated for their rights while they stayed in their countries, but its individual member states have systematically rejected their claims as soon as they left them. Hundreds of Romani asylum-seekers from Romania, Slovakia, and the Czech Republic saw their asylum applications rejected on the grounds that they were considered mere economic refugees. Four years ago, the Belgian authorities deported a group of 74 Roma asylum-seekers from Slovakia, for which Belgium was later condemned by the European Court of Human Rights for violating the prohibition against collective deportations in the European Convention on Human Rights. Only in a few instances has the plight of the region's Roma been acknowledged, such as in 2001 when France granted asylum to several Roma from the Hungarian village of Zamoly, where they had seen their houses demolished by the city council and been exposed to death threats.
© "EU Enlargement: European No Man's Land, The European Roma Information Office", Transitions Online, 10.05.2004

Modern media dictatorships allow large sections of the population to remain in the dark about their own deprivation of rights and lowered social status. In the flickering twilight of the tv lounge, that universal paralysis is produced that assists the process whereby ever more mysterious autocrats achieve popularity and obtain power.
© Popovic, Nenad, "A Copernician Turn", Eurozine, 03.04.2001

But the capital of Europe has filled a skip with its history and carted it off. If you arrive by car, you drive through new housing landscapes, uncultivated ground and a tunnel directly into the four-lane wind canals of the 'Europe Quarter'. If you use the train, you are greeted by the sooty walls of the central station. And if you set out from the metro station Maalbeck in search of the European Parliament, then you lose yourself in underpasses or on badly signposted escalators. The journey between missing paving stones and unsafe vacant lots is a nightmare. At the same time, it is in the glass cathedral, which now rises up here where the Brasserie Leopold once was, that all the lovely guidelines are decided upon – guidelines as to decent living conditions for handicapped people, for example.
© Weingärtner, Daniela, "The Union that ate up the town", taz, 24.06.2003

Bruges was once the New York of the 15th century, the heart of the Hanse, rich and beautiful. A little of its old splendour can still be gleaned from the classical manor house, which today houses the most important elite school in the European Union: The College of Europe, chamber of study to 270 young people from 40 countries, gives lessons in two languages, by 140 teachers from 25 nations.
© Fritz-Vannahme, Joachim, "Everything good comes from the East," DIE ZEIT, 18.03.2004

As of 1 May 2004, the Czech Republic, Slovakia, and the eight other new EU member states are obliged to implement the so-called Dublin II regulation. This regulation establishes which member state must assess asylum claims submitted in one of the 25 countries of the EU. In practice, the first EU state an asylum seeker enters is usually the one responsible for determining his refugee status. In the past, the Dublin Regulation achieved poor results owing to the difficulty obtaining evidence that the applicant was present in another EU state before submitting his asylum claim in a subsequent state. This changed significantly with the introduction in 2003 of the Eurodac system establishing a joint EU database of fingerprints and identification data. Together, these two EU regulations give member states a sound legal basis for sending asylum seekers to the countries of their first registration, whether Poland, Slovakia, Italy, Spain, or Greece. Disadvantages of the improved transfer regulation are obvious: Burden shifting instead of burden sharing; asylum seekers forced to return to countries where they may not wish to stay; and reception shortfalls in countries creating the external EU border. In addition, the costs of transfers, sometimes repeatedly of the same people, are very high.
© Rozumek, Martin, "EU Law: The Fiction of Harmonized Standards", Transitions Online, 08.12.2004

It is difficult to say how it will look in megalopolis and megalopolitan areas, especially in the poorer parts of the world. But let us take Europe and imagine two or three cities with twelve million inhabitants – they would "swallow" several small states. You know it is not possible. Fortunately! Sometimes it is confirmed that the division of Europe by small symbolic frontiers can be an advantage. Maybe I see it like this: My ideal Europe is the Europe of the 18th century. Europe contained many small states with symbolic frontiers. When we read Giacomo Casanova, we find that he travelled without a passport, probably sometimes only illegally. Each of these state formations had one city, a small metropolis, which was a large, strong cultural centre. When I think about Europe, I like to think not of the Europe of states, but the Europe of cities. At the same time, the city always acquires the characteristics of a state centre and national centre – in a very complex, but very good system. In urbanism, the more complex a system is the better.
© Abraham, Samuel, Bogdanovic, Bogdan, Marcelli Miroslav, "The architecture of the European city, Interview with Bogdan Bogdanovic", Eurozine, 20.10.2003

Central European cities such as Vienna, Budapest, Prague and perhaps also Bratislava are Danubian cities. It is as if they are all on the same street. I always repeat: We have stayed on the same street – the River Danube – we have only changed the number of our house a little. We have moved a little way further up the hill and up the river. The role of the Danube is not only symbolic, but real, and it is very important for me. The Danube is a

symbol. In the first years of our life here, when I was depressed - and there were reasons for this, since I had left my country - I went to the Danube and felt at home. And it applies in reverse. When Viennese friends, Professor Achleitner and Vienna television visited me last year in Belgrade, I took them to the Danube, although in Belgrade it is quite complicated, access to the Sava is easier. And it seemed to me as if they felt they were in Vienna. Only, perhaps this sounds like local patriotism, they were enchanted, because the Danube in Belgrade is much bigger than the Danube at Vienna. It is huge, almost like a sea. So the Danube is something symbolic. However, there is a small linguistic problem. The Danube is feminine in gender in German, she is a lady, but in Serbian, the river is masculine in gender, he is a young man, a hero, the River Sava is feminine.
... The Danube is also masculine in Slovak.
© Abraham, Samuel, Bogdanovic, Bogdan, Marcelli Miroslav, "The architecture of the European city, Interview with Bogdan Bogdanovic", Eurozine, 20.10.2003

"The Danube is at its lowest level since records began here in 1888," said Srdja Popovic, a Serbian environment ministry official. Rising in southern Germany and flowing almost through 10 countries to the Black Sea, the Danube is the second largest river in Europe and the key artery connecting the Balkans with central and western Europe. Four capital cities are built on its banks.
© Traynor, Ian, "Danube gives up trophies of war", The Guardian, 23.08.2003

One of the main areas of environmental concern in Central and Eastern Europe is Danube pollution. Seventeen countries with 165 million people all pour pollution into the Danube either directly or via five major tributaries. All seventeen countries contribute to this environmental crisis, but Romania is a worse offender than most. Although the Romanian government does want to clean up its bad track record on pollution, economic and political conditions are not conducive to success.
The Danube was once a thriving ecosystem and a centre of human daily life. It provided a communication and transportation system as well as food and employment. Today, it attracts raw sewage from cities, chemicals from agricultural run-off, waste from factories and bilge oil from ships. Much of this pollution is later washed up on coastal beaches, spreading disease and making them unsafe for residents and tourists alike. Chemicals in the water have killed much of the marine life and destroyed the Danube's fishing industry.
© Lovatt, Catherine, "Diversity: An der schoenen, braunen Donau", Transitions Online, 13.09.1999

The translation of the original "Balkan" into English yields an uncanny plural, "The Balkans", which is paradoxically closer to the true cultural multiplicity of that region. (Italian: Gli Balcani; Spanish: Los Balcanes; French: Les Balcanes, etc.) [...] This plural is symptomatic of Europe and its transatlantic extensions' inability to symbolize its own imaginary south-eastern region as a sovereign territory in a singular substantive form. The chaos and disorder imagined in the symbolic domain of this symbolic territory prevents the imaginary vision of the Balkans as a discursive formation sprouting from a single imaginary origin.
© Tomislav Longinovic, Balkan in Translation, Eurozine 2004-01-16

Popular music and its various metamorphoses are especially interesting: turbo folk and yugo-rock in Yugoslavia, chalga and folk music in Bulgaria, "manale" in Romania. In Bulgarian cities and villages, chalga music not only killed the old socialist popular amusements but also successfully replaced English and American rock and disco music in clubs and pubs. It represented a culture of enjoyment that opposed both the "post-protestant", globalist ethos of entering capitalism and the hollow slogans of official nationalism. It took elements from traditional "orgiastic" Balkan festivities, from obscene folklore, Turkish and Gypsy music, and from the new-born semi-criminal subculture and combined them with postmodern electronic synthesizers and rhythm boxes. The result is less a music of protest and trauma than a tricksterlike, comic and aggressive transformation. It turns the lowermost picture of the Balkans upside down and converts the stigma into a joyful consumption of pleasure forbidden by European norms and taste. Contrary to the traditional dark image, this popular culture arrogantly celebrates the Balkans as they are: backwards and Oriental, corporeal and semi-rural, rude, funny, but intimate.
© Kiossev, Alexander, "The dark intimacy: maps, identities, acts of identification", Eurozine, 19.05.2003

In the early 1990s, political contention and division emerged among different Croatian and Bosnian women's groups over the explanation of the mass rapes in Bosnia. Should we emphasize the "gender" or the "ethnic" dimension of this compound violence against women? The debate took place within a political context of induced nationalism and ethnic hatred. [...] Women were tortured and abused in many different ways in war zones: They were systematically raped, gang raped, held as slaves, bodily searched by male militias at check points, exploited by prostitution, or forced into prostitution because it was the only way to survive. Even United Nation soldiers in Bosnia visited the war brothels. The Bosnian Islamic Community pronounced raped women "shehids", or holy warriors. The Serbian Orthodox and Croatian Catholic churches appealed to women to give birth to more nationals.
© Kesic, Vesna, "Muslim women, Croatian women, Serbian women, Albanian women", Eurozine, 09.05.2003

The invisible (and often politically instrumental) border between the Habsburg and Ottoman Empires divides the peninsula even today. It does so not only in terms of politics and religion, but also in everyday life. [ ] Experts claim that Balkan cuisine descends from the Arab or Ottoman versions of Persian cuisine. Its "natural" borders (which coincide neither with the former empires nor with the contemporary nation states) can be drawn somewhere around Zagreb, where it abuts the mid-European front of chocolate cakes, sugary salads, and milky potages, while to the South, at Rijeka, it shades into Dalmatian/Mediterranean cuisine of frutti di mare, pizzas, and spaghetti. But the poor highlanders' cuisine, as well as the cuisine of various religious minorities and nomads remain outside this map; and the various national "cultivations", appropriations, and emblematisations of traditional cuisine demand a different history, different maps.
© Kiossev, Alexander, "The dark intimacy: Maps, identities, acts of identification", Eurozine, 19.05.2003

The final decision will be made during NATO's 28-29 June summit in Istanbul. NATO had originally hoped to

end the Stabilization Force (SFOR) mission in Bosnia in 1998, three years after the end of the bitter war for control of the former Yugoslav republic. The alliance prolonged its mission until 2000, citing unsatisfactory postwar security conditions. Since then, it has continued to expand its mandate on a yearly basis, with the latest mandate expiring at the end of this year. Michael Humphreys, the head of the European Commission delegation in Bosnia, says the potential transfer of authority from SFOR to the EU-led EUFOR would be an easy task and that the quality and quantity of EU troops would be the same as that of the NATO-led troops. Logistically, the transfer would in effect amount to little more than a cosmetic change, replacing the SFOR badges on the uniforms of 7,000 troops with EUFOR insignia. Seventy percent of SFOR's troops are from EU member states and would be reassigned to EUFOR immediately, if the mission is approved in Istanbul.
© Alic, Anes, "Bosnia: Mixed Euphoria", Transitions Online, 25.06.2004

"Take a look at this map," President Clinton urged the American public on the eve of March 24, 1999, as NATO pilots prepared for the first bombing raids against Yugoslavia. "Kosovo is a small place, but it sits on a major fault line between Europe, Asia and the Middle East, at the meeting place of Islam and both the Western and Orthodox branches of Christianity," he continued. "To the south are our allies, Greece and Turkey; to the north, our new democratic allies in Central Europe. And all around Kosovo there are other small countries..." Inviting his compatriots to examine the map of Southeastern Europe, an area that – he so obviously assumed – they were not overly familiar with, the American president chose some well known tropes of Balkan representation. In a seismological metaphor, he described the peninsula as a fracture zone, a clash-point of religions and civilizations. Kosovo and its surrounding "small countries" are – according to this presidential mini-lecture in Balkan political geography – uneasily sandwiched between Europe, Asia, and the Middle East, while at the same time separating America's old NATO allies from her new Central European friends. As is often the case, the Balkans are thus defined not by identity traits of their own but by their position on the fault line, their fate predetermined by their explosive "in-betweenness."
© Goldsworthy, Vesna, "Invention and in(ter)vention: The rhetoric of Balkanization', Eurozine, 08.05.2003

The EU should surely welcome members more convinced of the virtues of membership. But inviting Turkey could also have another benefit: It could make it easier to reject poor applicants. By opening talks with a country that seems un-European and so underdeveloped, the EU has effectively provided assurance that opponents of enlargement to the Balkans and the Black Sea will not be able to derail the enlargement project. Politically, that should make it easier to refuse or postpone entry to applicants unwilling to reform fast. At the moment, that chiefly means Romania, which last week received another bad report from the EU. If the EU refuses it membership in 2007, it will chiefly be Romania's fault; it will not necessarily be evidence that the EU is backtracking on the notion of enlargement. A larger, looser EU with Turkey might make some unhappy, but the rationale is familiar. The notion of an ever closer European union was born of fear of Germany. The possibility of an EU with Turkey has been revived by a fear of problems in the Middle East and the Black Sea. Moldova and Transdniester, Ukraine, and the south Caucasus all need greater stability. What they need now is to force change. With the status quo in Abkhazia and South Ossetia increasingly unsustainable, with elections in Moldova in February 2005 and two weeks away in Ukraine, now would be an excellent time for some of Europe's often forgotten countries to make a decisive break with their past. If they can achieve those huge tasks, they could then argue strongly that they should be the next Turkey, and that the EU should one day cross the Carpathians and the Black Sea.
© "The EU: Crossing the Bosphorus", Transitions Online, 11.10.2004

Over the last decade it is estimated that more than 2,500 would-be immigrants died trying to get into Europe. That is many dead, but not many immigrants for a continent of over 350 million people. Whom is it we are determined to keep out to the point that they risk their lives to get in: An equally determined but tiny minority of men, women and children from mostly poor countries who will come no matter what in search of work or refuge. They are not criminals. Yet the result of our determination is that we are feeding a criminal trade. There has been a sharp growth in illegal trafficking of people as receiving countries have clamped down on entries and semi-militarized more and more borders.
© Sassen, Saskia, "Is this the way to go?", Eurozine, 17.09.2002

Bands of refugee traffickers are profiting from human hardship. The IOM (International Organisation for Migration) has been talking for a long time of a "growth branch" that, according to the world migration report for this year, generates through careful management approximately 10 billion dollars annually.
© Krieger, Regina, "Images of overcrowded boats are deceptive", Handelsblatt, 04.08.2003

Two weeks after a severe boat accident with at least 36 fatalities, 10 more refugees have lost their lives off the coast of Spain. As the newspaper El Pais reported yesterday, 48 North Africans had set out on a rubber dinghy in the Mediterranean for three days without food or drinking water.
© "Drama off the coast of Spain, 10 refugees died", dpa, taz, 14.11.2003

Illegal immigrants do the dirty work in Europe. Sometimes they die doing it, like the Chinese cocklepickers who drowned wretchedly off the coast of England. Workers on England's bleak coast collect cockles for a starvation wage. The shell animals are regarded by gourmets in Spain and France as a much sought-after delicacy.
© Luyken, Reiner, "In the clutches of the "gangmaster" ", DIE ZEIT, 01.04.2004

Around 15 million Muslims live in the European Union today. A period of strong economic growth in the 60s of the previous century awoke the need for "guest workers" and a large new Muslim migration to Europe began. The new immigrants were happy at their opportunity.
© Ajami, Fouad, "Transportable Islam", DIE ZEIT, 07.04.2004

Two dead stowaways have been discovered in the Northern Spanish port of Aviles in the hold of a German

freighter. Both the young men had probably suffocated, the police announced. They were not carrying any papers. The "Tinsdal" had come from Morocco with a cargo of zinc blende.
© "Stowaways dead", dpa, taz, 04.02.2004

One of the most important examinations that the growing European Union must set itself in the coming years and decades will be the question: How do we pass the test of the challenge of immigration? If European societies grow into this task, future immigration will enrich and strengthen them. If they fail at it, they will forfeit a part of their prosperity and suffer from social tensions.
© Annan, Kofi, "On using migration", taz, 29.01.2004

One EU decree makes the provision that, from 2005, first a digital passport photograph and then a digital fingerprint is to appear in the passports of all EU citizens. The decree moreover wants to create the legal requisites with which to compile national central data files containing the biometric data of all citizens. As a future prospect, what could emerge from this is an EU central data bank.
© Winkelmann, Ulrike, "Whoever travels is under suspicion. Armaments of passports", taz, 21.05.2004

The president of the European Council of Jewish communities, Cobi Benatoff, yesterday lamented anti-Semitism in Europe at the conclusion of the general meeting in Budapest. Anti-Semitism must have reached unimaginable dimensions in the course of recent years. At the same time, Benatoff demanded that it should be combated with deeds rather than with words.
© "Anti-Semitism lamented", dpa, taz, 24.05.2004

On the site of the former German extermination camp, Belzec, in East Poland, it is expected that a museum planned as a memorial will open on 3 June. Within the space of ten months, just under half a million of Polish Jews above all were murdered by the National Socialists at Belzec in 1942. The names of the murdered are to be listed in the museum, as far as they are known.
© "Belzec memorial", dpa FAZ, 17.04.2004

At Auschwitz, Poland is not just having to adjust its understanding of the wartime sufferings of the Poles and Jews. It also has, somehow, to live with the reality that a German death camp for Jews in a Polish town is a site of huge international significance. For the town itself, it is a struggle to maintain an ordinary life while honoring the grim heritage imposed upon it by the Nazis. The town's daily routines and initiatives often come across as a lack of respect for the dead. That was the case when a discotheque was opened outside the protection zone but in a building that the SS used to store suitcases and the hair of those who had been sent to the gas chambers. That particular conflict was solved on legal grounds (the disco had to move), but it still put Poland back in the world's headlines, reminding everyone involved - the Polish government, the local authorities of Oswiecim (the Polish name for the town of Auschwitz), and the town's residents - that Auschwitz is not entirely an internal matter for Poland.
© Kosc, Wojciech, "Poland: Living with Auschwitz", Transitions Online, 02.02.2005

It was World War II. Romania was fighting alongside Germany in hopes of regaining territory that had been annexed by the Soviet Union. Jews were persecuted by Romania's fascist dictatorship, led by Marshal Ion Antonescu, and were accused of being communist sympathizers. They were murdered by the thousands in death trains and mass shootings, and they were deported to camps and ghettos in the country's newly reconquered territory in the northeast, then called Transnistria.
According to the Holocaust Encyclopedia, Romania had about 980,000 Jews in 1933. By 1950, the number was around 280,000. But that didn't stop the government of President Ion Iliescu from stating last year that the Holocaust had not happened in his country.
© Frye, Barbara, "Romania: Teaching the Holocaust", Transitions Online, 08.10.2004

In this article, I shall call the countries of the Vysegrad group (Poland, Hungary and the Czech Republic) Central Europe, and Ukraine, Belarus and Russia, Eastern Europe. I know that in Ukraine and Belarus there are many people who would disagree with this division. Nobody wants to be an Eastern European or Balkan country any more. On all the outskirts of the Pax Occidentis, politicians and intellectuals spend as much effort on region-imagining as they used to spend on nation-imagining. The success of the Hungarians', Poles' and Czechs' project of Central Europe as a "first-tier waiting-room" is too much of a temptation not to try to emulate. In Croatia and Slovenia, in Romania and Lithuania, in Belarus and Ukraine, many politicians and intellectuals are trying to prove that they are part of Central or East-Central Europe too. It's easy to understand them: Everybody wants to be rich and healthy rather than poor and sick. Today, Europe's political boundaries do not coincide with its geographic ones. The new boundaries of the successful and soon-united Europe run along the Eastern and Southern borders of Central Europe. To be part of Eastern Europe or the Balkans means being in a club of hopeless losers. Hundreds of books, articles and speeches about Ukraine's and Belarus's membership of European civilisation and the Central European region have been printed and held in these countries and in their Western neighbour, Poland, over the past ten years. What is the political meaning of these conceptions? The borders of Central Europe have always been drawn to two purposes. On the one hand, there is the desire to be included in the Pax Occidentis, and on the other hand, the desire to distinguish oneself from one's Eastern or Southern neighbour. In the case of Ukraine and Belarus, this motive is very important. It hides both a certain political calculation and a fear, or rather multiple fears, which are all linked to Russia in one way or another.
© Miller, Alexei, "Eastern Europe, Imagining Anew", Eurozine, 28.10.2002

Bulgaria lies without doubt in Europe, actually at the spot where it was born, if you want to see its identity in philosophy. Where the Thracians lived, where Orpheus was struck dead by ploughs, that he had not celebrated with his song and which therefore could injure him. But the West knows nothing of this country. For the 500,000 tourists on all-inclusive packages, who, as of recent times, besiege Sunny Beaches and Golden Sands on the Black

Sea every year, it remains a cheap alternative to Mallorca.
© Schmidt, Jochen, "Sofia on my mind", taz, 04.08.2003

Towards the north, one monstrous lump of a hotel after the other lines up along Mamaia, the tongue of land lying between the Black Sea coast and a lake. In the distance shimmers the silhouette of the oil refinery of Novodari, whilst right down to the water, the beach bars' jukeboxes leave scarcely a centimetre that isn't filled with sound.
© Meyer, Heiko, "Romania's Riviera is still asleep", taz, 13./14.11.2003

After a surprise visit to Iraq, U.S. Defense Secretary Donald Rumsfeld arrived in Constanta, Romania's main port on the Black Sea coast, some 250 kilometers east of Bucharest. He visited the Mihail Kogalniceanu air force base, which was used by U.S. forces during the Iraq war and is seen as the most likely location for a permanent U.S. presence in the region. Rumsfeld then left for Bucharest, where he met Romanian President Ion Iliescu. Sources in the Romanian Defense Ministry said Rumsfeld also visited another military facility on his way to the capital but refused to name it. "I can't say when and if U.S. forces will have a permanent base in Constanta. Moving the American military bases from Central towards Eastern Europe will be a gradual process for the next four to six years," Rumsfeld said after meeting with Romanian leaders. He thanked the Romanian army for its role in Iraq and Afghanistan and stressed that Romania was a powerful and reliable ally of the United States. "We've discussed concrete aspects of Romanian-American cooperation, including in the military area," Iliescu said. He confirmed that military bases were among these topics and stated that any decision should be made with parliamentary approval.
© Amariei, Razvan, "Gains and Pains From NATO", Transitions Online, 18.10.2004

The Danube Delta reserve is a 5,700-square-kilometer expanse of reeds, watery channels, pelicans, and birch and willow trees. No road network links its villages, and most transportation happens via boat. Some homes lack indoor plumbing. Digital phone service came only last year. In the last five years, researchers here have identified 27 species of plants and insects new to science. UNESCO, which added the region to its World Heritage List in 1991, called it the "largest and best preserved of Europe's deltas." It's a breeding ground for tens of thousands of birds and sometime-habitat of several threatened species. Post-Ceausescu restoration efforts have begun to show results. Since 1994, the reserve authority has reclaimed almost 10,000 hectares as wetlands (about one-eighth of the land that had been drained). Fish hatcheries have been set up, fishing has been more tightly regulated, and officials have cracked down hard on poachers. Industries upriver have closed down, and farmers are forbidden to use long-lived chemicals. As a result, some fish species that had disappeared from the Delta by 1990 have reappeared. In addition, the annual catch, which plunged from about 16,000 tons in 1986 to about one-quarter of that in 2000, has begun to level off. And the pelican population has increased to the point that there are now too many of the birds.
© Frye, Barbara, "Romania: Unquiet Flows the Danube", Transitions Online, 22.12.20.04

Inviting Turkey is a choice, not a necessity, for Europe - albeit one with strong strategic arguments to support it - and a choice that will be hard, ultimately maybe even impossible to reverse, however many referenda are called. Inviting Ukraine is also not a necessity, but a choice. A credible offer conditioned on tough but achievable reform steps could embolden liberals in Ukraine as it has done in Turkey, where it unleashed a stunning transformation that many observers thought unlikely, if not impossible, only a few years ago. The transformation of a richly endowed nation in a geographical position of huge importance would also help Europe. By contrast, dealing with the western Balkans - Croatia, Bosnia, Serbia and Montenegro, Albania, Macedonia - is a necessity, not a choice. The EU did not cover itself in glory during the 1990s when it responded in singularly uninspired fashion to the violence that tore Yugoslavia apart. Those days have thankfully passed, but it is by no means clear that the EU has a realistic strategic vision for Southeastern Europe today any more than it did 10 years ago.
© "The EU: The Reluctant Visionary", Transitions Online, 20.12.2004

The past year has produced three major changes in the EU's stance. First, in March 2004, Brussels agreed to allow Moldova to export tax-free to the EU products such as textiles and agricultural goods (though subject to some conditions), while allowing Moldova to protect its own market from EU products for up to seven years. Second, after years of Moldovan requests, the European Commission decided to open a delegation in Moldova, a diplomatic move similar to opening an EU embassy. Finally, on 8 February this year, Brussels said it would appoint a special representative for Moldova, a signal that the EU is preparing to play a more active role in the process of resolving the conflict in Transdniester, a region that broke away from Moldova after a short war in 1992.
© Popescu, Nicu, "Moldova & the EU: A Wind of Change", Transitions Online 02.03.2005

Another strong push behind the Czech interest in Ukraine was oil. The Galician oilfields potentially offered both a resource for Czech industry and an investment opportunity for Czech companies hoping to absorb German and Austrian owned oil enterprises. In April 1919, Czechoslovakia and the Western Ukraine People's Republic agreed on an oil-for-ammunition deal. Their diplomats even broached the idea of a future Czechoslovak- Ukrainian-Romanian-Yugoslav alliance aimed against Poland, Hungary and Austria. This somewhat far-fetched notion proved stillborn, and in any case Prague's attitude stemmed above all from economic interests, for at the same time the Czechs were selling arms to Poland and allowing French arms and ammunition to transit through Czech territory to Poland.
© Wojcik, Slawomir, "Galicia: After the Fall", Transitions Online, 11.02.2005

Europeans still think of themselves primarily in national terms; they have not yet developed the relations of trust and solidarity on the European level that would be necessary to underpin a stronger governing capacity.
© Offe, Claus, "The Democratic Welfare State", Eurozine, 08.02.2002

Out of the 75 million inhabitants of the EU member states, 67 million live in those five countries that until 1918 belonged wholly or partly to Austria-Hungary. That is approximately 90 per cent of the people who will become new EU citizens on 1 May.
© Bollmann, Ralph, "Kakanien in numbers", die tageszeitung, 24/25.04.2004

Every country has its East. Germany has the former GDR, while for East Germany on the other hand, the East is already in Poland. In Poland meanwhile, everything is Eastern that lies to the east of the Vistula; that is, poor and underdeveloped and Russian during the divided period. And in White Russia, there is also a West – the regions that once were Polish – as well as the (never not Russian) East.
© Rada, Uwe, "A marriage with obstacles", taz, 13.08.2003

Cross-border goods transport is already failing in the EU that is set at the present gauge because of the wide variety of platform, signal and electricity systems. Standardization was never important enough for the national governments. It is also for this reason that an alteration in the goods traffic along the tracks of east-west traffic is not to be expected to any extent worth mentioning any time soon.
© "Towards the east, there are still a lot of gaping holes in the road and rail network", enn, FAZ, 26.04.2004

Fear of rising prices after joining the EU has given rise to panic-buying in several of the ten new member countries over the past few days. Thus consumers in the Baltic states of Estonia, Latvia and Lithuania, as well as in Slovakia, have increased their stocking up on basic food stuffs like sugar, salt and flour.
© "Panic-buying in the states joining the EU", dpa, FAZ, 26.04.2004

The first sections of a 4 by 14 kilometre long oil carpet are expected today along the east coast of Sweden between Simrishamm and Ystad. [...] The 65 tonnes of calcium carbonate (potash) with which the "Fu Shan Hai" was on the way to China from the Latvian harbour of Ventspils – it was from here that in recent years the "Prestige" also set sail – threatened to intensify the problem of the overuse of fertilisers in the whole of the southern Baltic.
© "In the Baltic Sea, the cod are gasping for air", taz, 03.06.2003

50 European states would like to improve the health of children through a common plan of action. The themes range from combating obesity in west Europe to measures against air pollution in east Europe. Ministers and the World Health Organisation were in agreement on the paper.
© "Sick children in Europe. Taking action together", dpa, die tageszeitung, 28.06.2004

But it is no longer a national campaign that Cohn-Bendit is carrying out, his election battle is not just taking place in Germany or France. During these weeks, you can come across him over the whole of the continent, Madrid, Budapest, Paris, Dublin, Warsaw, Rome .... and Frankfurt, of course. It is the first European election campaign. It's visibly a lot of fun for its creator and main player, and, above all, for a few weeks it generates something like a European public. That is what Cohn-Bendit is dreaming of.
© Geis, Matthias, "France's Frankfurter", DIE ZEIT, 03.06.2004

The European Union has become bigger but not, however, more popular. The participation of its citizens in the election for the EU Parliament was the lowest there has ever been. Furthermore, the election success of Euro-sceptics points to the fact that populistic anti-EU politics have an increased currency.
© Lorenzen, Hannes, "Closing further up on Europe", taz, 12.07.2004

On the big screen next to the stage, one can meanwhile follow how a retinue made up of Schröder, Spidla and Miller crosses the bridge. "They can all say that they were there," insists the female presenter, then we hear Norah Jones, "You'll be on my side", while Schröder kisses a Sorbian girl.
© Gräff, Friederike, "Fried sausages against anxiety, from Zittau", taz, 03.05.2004

In Frankfurt on the Oder, what emerges from "borders in a state of flux" is in fact the border. Not just for Michael Zeller, who forgot his identity card but was quite lucky. The Federal Border Police play it cool – except in the case of Jurij Andruchowycz, the only Ukrainian author on board. Scarcely has the celebratory opening of the garden and the reading in the Kleist museum come to an end, than the company dispels. The Germans and the Dutch remain in Frankfurt on the Oder. The Poles, Jurij Andruchowycz and Michael Zeller are drawn to Polish Slubice, lying on the opposite side.
© Rada, Uwe, "Flowing identities", taz, 5./6.06.2004

Aurith is a village on a dyke. A handful of houses, two inns, a path along the bank. Behind it flows the Oder. Some days here, you feel as if you are on a lake. Because the river is wide whenever it is carrying a lot of water and the waves make it choppy. And also because you cannot make it over to the other side. An old ferry landing stage protrudes a hundred paces out into the Oder. From here, you can see red roofs behind willows, and the wind carries over the yapping of dogs. There is no way across with the ferry. The last ferry cast off in 1945.
© Veihelmann, Tina, "Where two worlds end", taz, 28.04.2004

In the Nordic Countries there was opposition on the right and on the left. The right was opposed for the usual reasons – nationalism, fear of migrants, contempt for southern Europe. But the left (or parts of it) have been opposed for quite different reasons. Europe, they said, would be an imperialist power vis-a-vis the Third World. Scandinavia, they said, was at least Social Democratic. A united Europe might be more fiscally conservative and threaten the welfare state; and Europe is insufficiently democratic. [...] Finally, there is a hidden racism, a sense of moral superiority vis-a-vis the continental Europeans.
© Wallerstein, Immanuel, "The Politics of Euroskepticism", Eurozine, 12.02.2001

Whoever desires more security should not build Europe up into a fortress. Whoever wants more security must seek out and cultivate the discussion. More and more expenditure on security, though, merely nurtures in us the illusion that we are safe. We no longer live in that period of time during which the most stoutly strengthened fortress guaranteed the best security. Fortresses only exist in our heads these days.
© Senocak, Zafer, "Goethe instead of Schily", taz, 24./25.04.2004

Europe has the world's highest suicide rate and cases are rising among young people, according to the World Health Organization (WHO). Dr Gudjón Magnusson, WHO director for Europe in charge of mental health, told SocietyGuardian.co.uk that Europe needed to lose its shameful record of 17.5 suicides per 100,000 population. He was speaking at a 52-country ministerial summit on mental health being staged in Helsinki. "There are 873,000 suicides worldwide and Europe, east and west, has 163,000 of those. There are probably 10-15 times that number of attempted suicides," he said. Of around 30 countries which gave data to the WHO, Lithuania had the worst rate at 44 suicides per 100,000, the UK nearly seven per 100,000 (higher than Italy and Malta) and the lowest number was in Azerbaijan at 1.41 per 100,000.
© O'Neill, Peter, "Europe is world's suicide hotspot", The Guardian, 14.1.2005

How thousands of Bulgarian workers used visa companies to sidestep the rules. Trendafil Tasev's "business plan" runs to around 70 pages in a blue folder lying on the desk of a small office on the fourth floor of a tenement in central Sofia. For the 30-year-old welder from the Bulgarian capital, the folder is more than a plan. It's a dream, the key to a new life on the building sites of London. "Trendafil Tasev is a very well-experienced welder who intends to start his own business in the UK," are the opening words of the bid to set up a one-man company in Britain called "Tasev-Welding". But first the blue folder has to go through the post all the way from Sofia to Yorkshire, where the Sheffield immigration office at the centre of the current immigration row will decide whether Mr Tasev's dream comes true. He has shelled out four months' wages, or £430, for the folder containing everything from an English translation of his welding certificate to tips on coping with the Inland Revenue and London Transport. And until this week, when an angry British consul in neighbouring Romania plunged the home secretary, David Blunkett, and his deputy Beverley Hughes into an ugly baiting match with the Tories over immigration from the Balkans, the blue folder was virtually certain to guarantee him an extendable one-year visa as a self-employed worker in the UK.
© Traynor, Ian, "Passports to prosperity: business plans that guaranteed a job in Britain", The Guardian,1.4.2004

The universal right of residence of EU citizens in all parts of the EU is valid everywhere – only not in Denmark.
© Feddersen, Jan, "Journeys through Europe (V)", taz, 30./31.08.2003

Although Latvia numbers 2.3 million inhabitants, officially only 1.9 million of those will become EU citizens. A fifth of the population is actually stateless. They have "Alien" – stranger – on their passports. The non-citizens, mainly of Russian origin, have practically the same status as the Latvians in everyday life, however they are barred from the right to vote or to stand for election, compulsory military service, as well as employment in the civil service.
© "The new members of the EU", NZZ, 26.04.2004

There is a summary of the most recent shifts in the European political landscape by Donald G. McNeil Jr. entitled "Politicians pander to fear of crime"(The New York Times, 5/6.05.2004). Indeed, throughout the world ruled by democratically elected governments, the "I'll be tough on crime" has turned to be the highest trump card that beats all others, but the winning hand is almost invariably a combination of "more prisons, more policemen, longer sentences" promises with "no immigration, no asylum rights, no naturalization" oaths. As McNeil puts it - "Politicians across Europe use the 'outsiders cause crime' stereotype to link ethnic hatred, which is unfashionable, to the more palatable fear for one's own safety".
© Bauman, Zygmunt, "A post-modern grid of the worldmap? Interview with Milena Yakimova, Eurozine, 08.11.2002

Modern history can be regarded as the attempts of Western civilization to Europeanize and to Westernize the world everywhere, with all the bad and good consequences. But only in Eastern Europe had this Westernization taken such deep roots that it became an essence of local identities. Without it, this space most likely would have remained a large and ambivalent Rus' (Ruthenian space),and not have differentiated into modern Russia, Ukraine, and Belarus. Eastern Europe is the only region beyond the West where the concept of the welfare state has been realized, albeit in the form of communism. If both the emergence and the dismantling of modern empires could be considered as a part of the European project, then Eastern Europe has made a significant contribution to it.
© Hrytsak, Yaroslav, "The borders of Europe seen from the outside", Eurozine 10.01 2005

The Parliament sits in Strasbourg, the committee meetings take place in Brussels, the administration resides in Luxembourg. In spite of this madness, members of parliament were until now unable to oppose the Council's stubborn strengths of persistence. All efforts to economize on costs with the move to Brussels failed – this year alone, they amount to 203 million Euros.
© Pinzler, Petra and Fritz-Vannahme, Joachim, "Softly and quietly towards power", DIE ZEIT, 09.06.2004

Yes, old Europe is infatuated with itself and its virtues. Can one remain virtuous for all eternity, however? Can one bring to perfection, unpunished, what already appears to be perfect? For almost half a century, this image has been missing a flaw, was without a crack. One can bravely assert that old Europe was so pre-occupied with itself that it didn't have any time left for transgressions. Appalled at its own past, it wanted at any price to win back its innocence.
© Stasiuk, Andrzej, "A view onto a soft, painless extermination", Süddeutsche Zeitung, 30.04./1./2.05.2004

Notes on contributors/Colophon

Maja Bajevic, artist, lives and works in Sarajevo and Paris.
Thierry Geoffroy, artist, lives and works in Copenhagen. www.colonel.dk
Ron Haselden, artist, lives and works in London and Plouer sur Rance. www.ronhaselden.com
Dan Mihaltianu, artist, lives and works in Berlin, Bergen and Bucarest.
Ulli Seegers, Dr. phil., art historian, lives and works in Cologne.
Tanya Ury, artist, lives and works in Cologne. www.youarewhy.com
Anu Vahtra, artist, lives and works in Tallinn.

Doris Frohnapfel, artist, lives and works in Cologne.
1998-2005 professorship at Bergen National Academy of the Arts in Norway.
Recent exhibitions: Illinois Art Institute Chicago; Encontros da Imagem Portugal;
Change + Partner Contemporary Art Rome; Kunstnernes Hus Oslo;
Fotogalleriet Oslo; Krings-Ernst Gallery Cologne.
Recent publications: "Replikk", Bergen University 2005,
"From Work to Word", Cologne/Bergen 2002;
"Norway and Wittgenstein", Cologne/Bergen 2000;
"Klack Klack", Cologne/Bergen 2000.
Contact: frohnapfel@netcologne.de

"Border Horizons" takes place in different formats
– DVD slide show, book, series of photographs, photo-video installation –
at the following venues:

"Shot Stories", 25.2. - 2.4.2005
M29 Richter • Brückner, Cologne, Germany

"Projekt Migration", 30.9.2005 - 15.1.2006
Kölnischer Kunstverein, Cologne, Germany

"Tracing Space", 24.11.2005 - 8.1.2006
Bergen Kunsthall, Bergen, Norway

"Border Horizons", March - June 2006
Krings-Ernst Gallery, Cologne, Germany

Bergen National Academy of the Arts' (KHiB)
intention is to focus on artistic research and
development. A program has been established to
encourage and investigate research practices in the
fields of Fine Art, Design and Applied Art. Through a
series of publications KHiB contributes to the debate
and development in contemporary visual art and arts
education.
ISBN 82-8013-047-0 (Norway)

k:

KUNSTHØGSKOLEN
I BERGEN

Bibliografische Information Der Deutschen Bibliothek
Die Deutsche Bibliothek verzeichnet diese Publikation
in der Deutschen Nationalbibliografie; detaillierte
bibliografische Daten sind im Internet über
http://dnb.ddb.de abrufbar.

ISBN 3-89770-241-X

www.salon-verlag.de
salon-verlag@netcologne.de

Production: Heinrich Miess, Cologne, Germany
Translation: Jean Bernis, London, England
Printing: Druckhaus Locher, Cologne, Germany

Printed in Germany
1000 copies and a special edition of 50 + 10 a.p.